Henry Rooke

Travels to the Coast of Arabia Felix

And from thence by the Red Sea and Egypt to Europe...

Henry Rooke

Travels to the Coast of Arabia Felix
And from thence by the Red Sea and Egypt to Europe...

ISBN/EAN: 9783744764612

Printed in Europe, USA, Canada, Australia, Japan

Cover: Foto ©Andreas Hilbeck / pixelio.de

More available books at **www.hansebooks.com**

TRAVELS

TO THE COAST OF

ARABIA FELIX:

AND FROM THENCE BY THE

RED-SEA AND EGYPT,

TO

EUROPE,

CONTAINING A SHORT ACCOUNT OF AN

EXPEDITION

UNDERTAKEN AGAINST THE

CAPE OF GOOD HOPE.

IN A SERIES OF LETTERS

By HENRY ROOKE, Esq;

LATE MAJOR OF THE 100th REGIMENT OF FOOT.

LONDON:
Printed for R. BLAMIRE, in the Strand;
Sold by B. LAW, Ave-Mary Lane; and
R. FAULDER, New Bond Street.

M DCC LXXXIII.

CONTENTS.

LETTER I.

Departure from Spithead — Island of Madeira — Trade Winds — Cape de Verd Islands — Anchor in Porto Praya — Description of St. Jago and the Town of Praya.

LETTER II.

Attack made by Monsieur Suffrein — Disadvantages under which the British Fleet laboured — Enemy beat off — English Fleet gives chase.

LETTER III.

Departure from St. Jago — Cross the line — Trinidada — Object of the Expedition publickly notified — Capture of Dutch Ships in Saldanha Bay — Attack of the Cape judged inexpedient — Commodore returns to England — Arrival at Joanna.

LETTER IV.

Description of the Island of Joanna — Visits paid by the Princes to the different Ships — Good accommodations procured for us by the Dukes — Singular worship addressed to Birds — Flying Fox or African Bat — Prepare to sail.

LETTER V.

Sickness in the Fleet — How accounted for — Fair Breeze for some time — Long Calm — Contrary Monsoon sets in — Put into Morebat Bay — Description thereof and of the Country — An Arabian Drawing-Room — Hookah — Fleets of Coasting Vessels.

LETTER VI.

Passage to Mocha — Description of that City — Kingdom of Sunnaa — Military Genius of the Arabians — Exercise of the Cavalry — Gentoos — Champooing — Oppressive Government.

LETTER VII.

Passage to Hodeida — Isle of Camaran — Battle with the Budoos — Cruelty of the Lascars — Touch

Touch at Confidah — Arrive at Juddah — Defcription of that place.

LETTER VIII.

Turkifh Coffee Fleet — Their curious mode of Navigation — Journal kept on board the Mahaboube — Arrival at Suez.

LETTER IX.

Journey over the Defert to Grand Cairo with a Caravan — Wretched fate of fome Englifh Merchants — Cruelty of the Government of Cairo towards them — Firman of the Grand Signor — Unpleafant manner in which the Chriftians are treated at Cairo.

LETTER X.

Excurfion to the Pyramids — Their Size — Apartments in the largeft — Sphynx — Situation of the antient City of Memphis — Ifland of Rhoida — Mikeaz — Ceremony of the opening of the Chalitz — Defcription of Cairo and the form of Government there.

LETTER XI.

Unpleafant Adventure with Muftapha Bey — Good Offices of Mr. R.——— — Interpofition

viii CONTENTS.

-tion of Ibrahim Bey — The Paſſage by Suez moſt favorable for ſending Intelligence to India — Arabian Concert — Nightly Police of the City.

LETTER XII.

Paſſage down the Nile to Roſetta — Annual overflow of that River — Fertility of Lower Egypt — Roſetta — Caſtle of Bekier — Nicopolis — Alexandria — Ruinous ſtate of the antient City — Pompey's Pillar — Cleopatra's Obeliſk — Baths — Pharos — Alexander's Body preſerved there to the time of Auguſtus.

LETTER XIII.

Sail from Alexandria — Touch at Rhodes — Deſcription thereof — Archipelago — Iſland of Candia — Tunis — Antient City of Carthage — Ciſterns — Aquædu&ct; — Embark for Leghorn — Arrival there.

TRAVELS

TO THE

COAST of ARABIA FELIX, &c.

LETTER I.

Porto Praya, April 13, 1781.

DEAR FRIEND,

THE guefs proved right which you formed when I parted with you on the Beach at Portfmouth and the next morning's light brought with it a favorable wind. What a glorious fight was the confequence! near forty fhips of the line with above an hundred others getting under way, the breeze frefh, the morning clear and pleafant; did you ever behold fo noble a fpectacle? perhaps it might ftrike *me* more forcibly, who was in the midft midst of that busy scene than you who was, I suppose, a spectator of it from the Ramparts: I beheld it with a degree of enthusiasm; those stupendous bulwarks managed with so much art, such regularity in the midst of so much apparent confusion, the alacrity of my brave companions who' were going forth to assert their own and their country's honor, the glorious events which so fine a force might produce; these and a thousand other reflections of the like nature were occasioned by this sublime sight.

The grand fleet destined for the relief of Gibraltar kept on it's course, while our little squadron brought up at St. Helen's for a few hours; the Commodore then made known his command by hoisting a broad pendant, which could not fly when an Admiral's flag was in sight: we weighed again in the afternoon and proceeded down Channel: The wind continued fair and passing the Lizard Lights on the third evening after our departure from Spithead we entered the Bay of Biscay famous for its storms, but found it of a more mild nature than we expected and had very little interruption to our good weather 'till we arrived off the Island of Madeira, when it became squally and tempestuous, and we then passed two or three very uncomfortable days: all our little amusements, so necessary to cheat the tedious hours on board of ship, were at a stop;

stop; our card-table could not stand, the chessmen were swept off the board, we could neither read nor walk; our dinners exhibited scenes distressing and ludicrous; in short you can conceive nothing so unpleasant as the involuntary motions one must submit to in a gale of wind: I found my cot the best resource and spent most of my time in it till the fair weather returned; which, after three days sufferings, we regained, and soon afterwards on coming within the tropick met with the trade winds, that blow always regularly and in the same direction. This phænomenon of the winds, which produces effects so useful to navigation and so pleasing to the mariner, is accounted for by philosophers on the principle of the sun and earth's compound motion, as Dr. Halley and Sir Isaac Newton can best explain to you. Having now a constant fair breeze and smooth water, our voyage became extremely pleasant: we quickly arrived at the Cape-de-Verd Islands, and brought up in this Bay after a passage of four weeks from England. Water and refreshments are the objects that have brought the fleet hither, of which we find a more plentiful supply than was expected: since the Commodore doubting whether there would be sufficiency for the whole, has sent a part to the Isle of May, situated ten leagues to windward of this.

St. Jago, the island off which we are now anchored, is the principal of the Cape de Verds: they were discovered in 1449 by Antonio Nolli, a Genoese, in the service of Portugal, and are ten in number, laying between 15 and 17 N. L. 18 and 20 W. L. from London; they abound in most tropical productions, but from the indolence of the natives and bad management yield very little: the exclusive trade to them and likewise to the coast of Guinea is vested in a company at Lisbon, who pay an annual sum to the government, but not sufficient for the expence of maintaining the forts and garrisons, as the wretched condition of them seems to indicate. The chief town of the island is situated close to the sea, and is ten miles distant from this place; the road that leads to it is very narrow and stony, up and down craggy hills, along which a jack-ass or poney conveys one with tolerable safety. The face of the country presents an appearance of brown parched and barren hills, seeming to have been formed by lava and volcanic fire; most of them terminate in a point like the *apex* of a volcano; the vallies are fertile and if cultivated would amply repay the pains of the husbandman: at present they produce trees and shrubs of various kinds, which grow spontaneously, such as the cocoa-nut, tamarind, orange, guava, lime, plantane, &c. but the plant of most consequence is madder, growing in great abundance among the cliffs.

You

You defcend to the town of St. Jago down the declivity of a mountain, almoft perpendicular, by a rugged and zig-zag path, with a precipice on each fide; the town ftands encompafs'd by hills towards the land; it feems to have been formerly a place of confequence, but is now in a ruinous and defolate condition, with few other inhabitants but negroes and no trade; the blacks came originally from the coaft of Guinea, and are very tall and robuft: they adorn themfelves with a profufion of beads, which they wear in form of necklaces and bracelets, and in their ears large gold and filver rings. The cathedral has a refpectable appearance, ftanding very boldly on a cliff that overhangs the fea; there is likewife a convent of Capucins, a pretty good building and pleafantly fituated; the holy fathers place before ftrangers who vifit them the beft cheer their houfe affords.

Allow me to bring you back from the capital to the town of Praya, compofed of a few mud hovels, ftanding on a cliff above the landing place; a battery of rufty guns and a flag-ftaff conftitute it a fort; the officer who commands here is what the Portugueze call a *Capitano Mor*; he is a kind of commandant and directs the police, militia, and revenue. In the valley below the town of Praya are two wells, from whence our fleet is watered; they yield a pretty copious

copious supply thereof, though it is rather of an indifferent quality; the furthest well from the sea produces the best; other refreshments are likewise plentiful here, such as bullocks, goats, hogs, poultry, eggs, oranges, plantanes, cocoa nuts and other fruits; these the natives bring to market, and exchange for old clothes, shirts, blankets, &c. commodities they value more than specie; from this traffic, which they carry on with all strangers that touch here, you see the fashions of almost every nation in Europe display'd in the coats, hats and other parts of the dresses of these negroes, who make rather a fantastical appearance from the variety and shabbiness of their European habiliments. This valley is thickly planted with cocoa nut, tamarind, and other trees, forming a pleasant grove; and intersperfed amongst them are several officers tents; great numbers of soldiers and sailors are on shore to fill the water-casks and buy provisions; our fair countrywomen make it their *Promenade* and enliven the scene. An house belonging to the Lisbon Company is on the verge of the grove and extremely convenient for our *Fêtes*; amidst the conviviality of which we forget the savage aspect of the land we are on and bear more patiently the raging heat of a vertical sun. As our ships, which were sent to the Isle of May are expected to join us here to-morrow, we shall most probably sail from hence
on

on the following day—You may suppose we are not a little anxious to know our destination: wherever it is, I am persuaded we have your best wishes for success and a prosperous campaign. Adieu.

LETTER

LETTER II.

Porto Praya, May 1, 1781.

DEAR FRIEND.

OUR campaign has opened somewhat sooner than we expected. While at anchor under the sanction of the Portugueze flag we thought ourselves equally secure from insult as if at St. Helen's, we were suddenly attack'd by a French squadron in a manner we little dreamed of and for which we were by no means prepared.

The point of this Bay to windward being high land and stretching pretty far out conceals from us every thing approaching on that side 'till it comes very near: under cover of this blind the enemy advanced, nor did we suspect the mischief that thus threatened us till on drawing near the point they opened to the Isis, which lay the furthest out in the Bay, and she

she immediately made the signal for discovering strange ships. They proved to be a French fleet under convoy of five sail of the line and a corvette, commanded by Monsf. de Suffrein, *Chef d'Escadre*, and were composed of the Heros and Hannibal of seventy-four guns each, the Sphynx, Artesien, and Vengeur all of sixty-four; they advanced very fast on our squadron with a great deal of sail set, and being gallantly lead by their Commodore into the center of our fleet began to engage us. Monsf. Suffrein in the Heros came to an anchor, as did the Hannibal his *matelot*; a spirited proceeding this, you'll say, to bring up in the midst of an enemy's fleet; but I fancy he made his calculations on surprizing us, and the event justified them. The conduct which the other three ships observed I cannot account for, unless finding our Indiamen on the outside they mistook them at first for men of war, though in that they must soon have been undeceived: I should think they would have co-operated more effectually with their Commodore, had they, like him, come to an anchor and directed all their efforts against our men of war; a plan more worthy of them than that of sailing about in the out-skirts of the fleet and making attacks on the Indiamen, in one of which only they succeeded, boarding and carrying out with them the Hinchingbrooke; but in an attempt of the like nature on the Fortitude were gallantly beat off, and met with a vigorous refiftance from moft of the others: had they, owing to the aukward fituation and unprepared ftate of our men of war, been able to make any impreffion on them, the convoy muft have fallen of courfe. You will fuppofe that the two French fhips in the midft of our fleet had a pretty warm birth, they were the objects for almoft every one to fire at, and not a fingle victualler that mounted fix four-pounders but directed them that way: from fo general a fire they fuffered confiderably, and after ftanding the brunt of it for near two hours retired from the fight much fhattered; the Hannibal was particularly ill-treated, and in its retreat had fcarce clear'd our fleet before her three mafts and bowfprit went overboard; fhe was indeed a compleat wreck; her companions bore down to her affiftance, and one of them took her in tow: we agreed that it would have been a more pleafing fight to have beheld an Englifh man of war perform that charitable office: the French then went off to leeward after their convoy.

We have to lament fome of our friends who fell in the action, and about two hundred men killed and wounded; a lofs, I fancy, far inferior to that of the enemy, who made their attack with great fpirit, it muft be confefs'd, but at the fame time with little judgment, the want of which on their parts, with firmnefs and exertion on ours, united

to

to save us in a position so extremely disadvantageous. Many of our ships had not above half their complement on board: the fleet was anchor'd without any order or regularity, merchantmen on the outside, men of war within; not above one or two had time to get springs on their cables, and lay likewise so much in each other's way that some could not bring their guns to bear upon the enemy and others in the confusion fired upon their friends.

How different this from what might have been the case if we had paid attention to the intelligence received on shore and made proper arrangements. We found by the Port book at Praya, (containing the names, countries, and descriptions of all ships arriving here) that a French frigate came into the Bay to water but a few weeks before and apprized the inhabitants of this fleet which she said would touch at Praya to refresh in the course of the month of April, desiring them to have cattle and every thing ready; and the people of the island so fully expected the French fleet, that when ours appeared they concluded it to be that of which the frigate had given them notice. All this we learned on our arrival, and had we in consequence thereof kept a look out to windward, had our men of war been moor'd head and stern with springs on their cables and formed in a line on the outside the convoy being within; had all our people been on board and the ships properly clear'd for action for which they would in that case have received timely notice, it is to be presumed that we should have been able to have given a better account of our own success and the enemy's loss: but who could suppose that the French, famous for their faith and their *etiquette*, would violate the neutrality of a Port and attack us laying supinely at anchor under protection of the Portugueze flag? I marvel much whether these violators of the law of nations would have scrupled to have taken our ships, had they found them in the disjointed state they were in but a day or two before, when half were watering at the Isle of May, the other half in Porto Praya; and when thus separately attacked they could have made but a feeble defence and the greater part must inevitably have fallen. A manifesto from the Court of Lisbon might have been the consequence, but I hardly think it would have procured restitution.

I should be glad to give you the sequel of this history, but having told you that in about two hours after the enemy had retreated in a confused and shattered condition, our men of war went out of the Bay seeming in good order and were saluted on all sides by the cheers and acclamations of a brave and spirited fleet, in which I dare say there was not a man who did not envy them that victory he trusted they were about to gain: I say after telling you

you this, allow me to draw a veil over what followed, and confign to oblivion St. Jago and our atchievements off that ifland; the gazette will probably explain the remaining tranfactions of the day and I leave you to your own comments on the occafion. Adieu.

LETTER

LETTER III.

Joanna, one of the Comora Islands.
Sept. 3, 1781.

DEAR FRIEND,

WHITHER have you now conducted me! Methinks I hear you exclaim on reading the date of this. Where is this same Joanna, and these Comora Islands from whence you now announce yourself? In what quarter of the globe are they? or, in what corner of my map can I discover them? Thus will you question me, if you are not better acquainted with their situation than I was till of late. Know then, that they are islands in the Indian Ocean, whose longitude is 45° east from London, latitude 12° south; are five in number, Joanna, Mayotta, Mohilla, Angazeia and Comora; that we have now touched here to take in water and refreshments in our way to India, where we are bound. By what means, and

COAST OF ARABIA FELIX, &c

and through what adventures we have paffed on to this length, the event of our fecret expedition, &c. you fhall briefly learn.

After leaving St. Jago our fancies and wifhes were continually employed in devifing what could be the object of our expedition and flattering ourfelves with a fpeedy accomplifhment of it. The two places between which our thoughts vibrated were Buenos Ayres, and the Cape of Good Hope; it proved to be the latter; of that we were fully certified on making the ifland of Trinadada fituated in latitude 20° fouth, longitude 29° weft from London. We arrived off that ifland after a month's paffage from St. Jago; when near the line we had much calm, and the weather was exceffively hot, the thermometer being generally 88. our people of courfe were beginning to grow fickly; however, in about 4° north we met with the fouth-eaft trade wind, which prevails in the fouthern tropick, and frefhening by degrees it revived us from the languor occafioned by the calm and fultry weather fending us acrofs the equinoctial line May 20th. This event produced the ufual ceremony of ducking fuch as had never before paffed it which is performed by a tackle fixed to the main yard arm, by means whereof the perfon ducked is lowered into the fea and there plunged three times; but the forfeit of a bottle of brandy exempts thofe who do not chufe chuse to undergo the discipline; the crew amuse themselves with various sports on this occasion, to which the grog arising from forfeits much contributes. Trinidada had been appointed a place of rendezvous in case of separation, but all our ships had kept together, and on our arrival there the object of the expedition was publickly notified. The Cape of Good Hope now engrossed the whole of our thoughts and conversation, we looked forwards to it with pleasure as the period of our voyage, formed our different plans of attack and flattered ourselves that a few weeks would put us into possession of that delightful settlement; but vain were all our hopes, and the evil genius that visited us at St. Jago came again across us and forbad our entrance into False Bay, as the sequel shall explain.

On the twelfth of June the Commodore sent forwards two frigates and two cutters to reconnoitre the Cape, examine the posture of defence of the enemy and discover whether the French squadron was arrived there; these, on their passage took an outward-bound Dutch Indiaman which had just left Saldanha Bay and was bound to Ceylon; from the accounts received thereby and letters found on board, it was discovered, that the French fleet arrived in False Bay on the 21st of June; that they had even brought the
shattered

shattered Hannibal with them by great exertions, having towed her most part of the way; that all necessary preparations were made for our reception and they were in daily expectation of the visit.

The resolution formed in consequence of this intelligence was, not to attempt the Cape; and our famous expedition, from which so much was expected, tamely terminated in the capture of some Dutch Indiamen that we surprized in Saldanha Bay on the twenty-first of July: they attempted to set fire to their ships, but succeeded only in burning one; most of the people made their escape on shore, a few only coming over to us among whom were two distinguished personages, no less than a King and the Prince his son, who threw themselves on our protection, rejoiced at having gained their liberty after a captivity of sixteen years on Robin Island laying near that coast. Their crime against the Dutch was, the having opposed them at Ternate one of the Moluccas, of which the old man was king. As we had been expected at the Cape for some time before, these royal captives were sent on board the Indiamen we took to be conveyed to Holland; those very ships had also been sent round from the Cape into Saldanha Bay as a place of security during the expected attack; it was from the prize taken at sea that we gained intelligence of them.

Saldanha is perhaps one of the fineſt Bays in the world; it branches into three or four, the inner one where the prizes were laying is called Hotties Bay; it is compleatly land-lock'd, ſecure, and large enough to contain two or three hundred ſail: the ſurrounding country is formed by wild uncultivated hills and plains covered thick with ſhrubs, the only inhabitants thereabouts are tygers, antelopes, deer, and quantities of game: did it but yield good water, it would be a more eligible place than the Cape for ſhipping and refreſhments, but the want thereof is the reaſon that no ſettlement has been formed there.

The whole country being one continued ſhrubbery preſents an extenſive field for the reſearches of a botaniſt; there are a vaſt number of plants growing wild which are foſtered with much care in Engliſh green-houſes; the air was perfumed with their fragrance; the climate is as ſoft and mild as that of Montpellier or Naples, for though it was the depth of winter, the air was quite clear, and ſun extremely warm, the thermometer being at 60. but we were allowed only a ſhort time to enjoy the pleaſures of this ſhore and climate, quitting it after a three days ſtay and regretting much that our viſit to the ſouthern promontory of Africa was of ſo tranſitory a nature, where our imaginations had painted to us the acquiſition of ſome honour and much pleaſure. By all

ac-

accounts it is a delightful settlement. The Cape Town is represented to be neatly and regularly built: the adjacent country mountainous towards the sea, but in land beautifully diversified with villas, vineyards, and plantations, the climate remarkably fine, and favorable to fruits and vegetables of all kinds, which, as well as every other sort of provisions, are extremely plentiful. The inhabitants are hospitable, of plain and easy manners, and much attached to the English, with whom they are greatly connected in time of peace, as our Indiamen generally touch there for refreshment, and in that point of view only it would have been a most desirable acquisition to us, and I fear we shall have great reason to regret the failure of this expedition during our war with the Dutch.

The Commodore continued with us for two or three days only after we left Saldanha Bay and then returned to England, taking with him two fifties and two frigates, the rest of the force is proceeding to India; and in our way thither we have touched here for water and refreshments, having been four months on our passage from St. Jago. This island appears very pleasant and inviting, in fact it is land, and *that* is no small recommendation. I mean to visit it to-morrow and shall defer a more particular account till my next. Adieu.

LETTER IV.

Joanna Town, September 23, 1781.

DEAR FRIEND.

THOUGH this is not the largeſt yet it may be reckon'd the principal of the Comora Iſlands; it claims ſovereignty over and exacts tribute from all the others: theſe pretenſions it is however ſometimes obliged to aſſert by the ſword and at preſent meditates an expedition againſt Mayotta which is in a ſtate of rebellion; the natives on being aſked the cauſe of their war with that people, reply "Mayotta like America:" they get their ſupplies of arms and ammunition from ſhips that touch here, and the arrival of ſo large a fleet as the preſent will prove very ſeaſonable to them, as it is cuſtomary for all to make preſents of arms and powder to the Prince when he pays a viſit on board which he does to every one; a ſalute is the compliment due on that occaſion,

but

but as our guns are shotted an apology is made for the omission of that ceremony, and the Prince readily admits of it provided he receives a number of cartridges equal to the guns that would have been fired.

The King lives at a Town about twelve miles off on the east side of the island, two Princes of the blood reside here; on going their round of visits they fail not to ask for every thing they see which strikes their fancy, and of course the honor of making a present to a Prince, induces one at first readily to grant what they request; but no sooner is that done than they make fresh applications till we are reduced to the rude necessity of putting the negative on most of them. These great personages are very richly dressed and attended by a numerous suite of slaves, who like their princely masters are much struck with the objects they see but use less ceremony in their manner of obtaining them: These black Princes (for that is the complexion of them and all the inhabitants) have by some means or other obtained the titles of Prince of Wales and Prince Will; the former has, I suppose, been jocosely called so by some Englishmen as being the heir apparent and the natives have adopted the term, not the only one they borrow from us; they have an officer stiled Purser Jack who seems to be at the head of the finance-department; of dukes they have a prodigious

digious number, who entertain us at their hotels for a dollar per day and give us for dinner very good rice and curry; thefe noblemen, together with a numerous tribe of others of all ranks, make the earlieft application to every one to follicit the honor of his company and cuftom, even before the fhip has let go its anchor they come along fide in their canoes and produce written certificates of their honefty and abilities from thofe who have been here before, the purport of which is to inform you that the bearer has given them good cheer, wafhed their linen well and fupplied their fhip punctually with all forts of refrefhments. The effect is ftriking and fingular on entering the road to fee a vaft number of canoes which are made of trunks of trees hollowed out with three or four black fellows in each; their faces turned towards the front of the canoe; with paddles formed like a fpade, digging away in the water and moving with no fmall velocity: to keep thefe cockle-fhells fteady and prevent them from over-fetting, they have what is termed an out-rigger, it is compofed of two poles laid acrofs the upper part of the canoe and extending feveral feet beyond the edges thereof on each fide, joined at the extremities by two flat pieces of wood, fo that it appears like a fquare frame laid acrofs the canoe: they are very long but fo narrow that one perfon only can fit breadthways. The price of every article here is
regulated

regulated and each ſhip has it's contractor who engages to ſupply it with neceſſaries at the eſtabliſhed rate, but I believe it is in many caſes exceeded by the great demand and the eagerneſs of half-ſtarved people to obtain freſh ſtock.

We find no other animals for our ſea proviſions but bullocks, goats and fowls, the ſeaſon for oranges is paſt, but we get moſt other tropical fruits and whatever we want, have only to give in a liſt to a duke and he provides us therewith: This, you will ſay, is a new character for a duke to appear in and ſuch it ſeems to be, but it is in fact only owing to the mode, they are their own ſtewards and diſpoſe of the produce of their eſtates themſelves, which noblemen of other countries do by the intermediate aid of an agent: they at leaſt act conſiſtent with their characters by an urbanity of manners which one is ſurprized to meet with in a people inhabiting a ſmall ſpot ſecluded from the reſt of the civilized world. They have a regular form of government and exerciſe the Mahometan religion ; both were introduced by Arabians who paſſed over from the continent and ſubdued the country; the original Joanna natives are by no means thoroughly reconcil'd to this uſurpation and ſtill look upon their conquerors with an evil eye. Like their ſentiments ſo are the colours of theſe two races of men very different, the Arabs have not ſo deep a tinge as

the

the others, being of a yellowish copper complexion with better features and a more animated countenance, they confider a black streak under the eyes and black teeth as ornamental, the former they make every day at their toilettes with a painting brush dipt in a kind of ointment, the latter is principally caused by the chewing of the betel nut: this custom which prevails in all Eastern countries answers to the fashion of smoking tobacco or taking snuff with us, except that with them it is more general, no one is without a purse or bag of betel and it is looked on as a piece of civility to offer it to your friend when you meet him or take leave; it is a small nut of the size of a filberd that grows on a creeping plant like a vine; together with the betel nut are chewed the leaves of the areca (a kind of palm tree) and a small quantity of *chinam* or lime, made of calcined shells, is added.

Their religion licenses a plurality of wives and likewise concubines; they are extremely jealous of them and never allow any man to see the women, but female strangers are admitted into the Harem, and some English ladies, whose curiosity has lead them there make favourable reports of their beauty and richness of apparel displayed in a profusion of ornaments of gold, silver, and beads, in form of necklaces bracelets

lets and ear-rings, they wear half a dozen or more in each through holes bored all along the outer rim of the ear.

'The men seem not to look with an eye of indifference on our fair countrywomen notwithstanding they are of so different a complexion; one of the first rank among them being much smitten with an English young lady wished to make a purchase of her at the price of five thousand dollars, but on being informed that the lady would fetch at least twenty times that sum in India, he lamented that her value was so far superior to what he could afford to give.

These people are very temperate and abstemious, wine being forbidden them by the law of Mahomet, but that prophet seems to have had less compassion on his followers when he enjoined them the fast of Ramazan, lasting for a month, during which they never taste of any thing from sun-rise to sunset; it is now about half over and with surprize we see them every day toiling in the heat of the sun, nor will the greatest thirst they can suffer justify the bare wetting the lips. They are frequent in prayer, attending their mosques three or four times a day; we are allowed to enter them on condition of taking off our shoes. These buildings are regular but quite plain; in prayer they prostrate themselves on the ground frequently kissing it and expressing very fervent devotion: the computation of time (which is dated from their prophet Mahomet) is termed the Higera, of which the prefent year is the 1195th; their new year begins September 14th: but I need not trouble you with a recital of all the laws of the Alcoran which you have moſt likely read.

The town from whence I date this is cloſe to the ſea, ſituated at the foot of a very high hill, and about a mile and a half in circuit; the houſes are incloſed either with high ſtone walls or palings made with a kind of reed, and the ſtreets are little narrow alleys, extremely intricate and forming a perfect labyrinth; the better kind of houſes are built of ſtone within a court-yard, have a portico to ſhield them from the ſun, and one long and lofty room where they receive gueſts, the other apartments are ſacred to the women; the ſides of their rooms are covered with a number of ſmall mirrors, bits of china ware and other little ornaments that they procure from ſhips which come here to refreſh: the moſt ſuperb of them are furniſhed with cane ſophas covered with chintz and ſattin mattreſſes: moſt of the people ſpeak a little Engliſh, they profeſs a particular regard for our nation and are very fond of repeating to you that "Joanna-man and Engliſh-man all brothers," and never fail to aſk " how King George do?" In general they appear to be a courteous and well diſpoſed people and very fair and honeſt in their dealings, though there are amongſt them as in all other nations ſome viciouſly inclined and theft

is

is much practifed by the lower clafs, notwithftanding the punifhment of it is very exemplary, being amputation of both hands of the delinquent.

The inhabitants of this ifland, like thofe of moft hot and tropical countries, are indolent and do not improve by their labour the richnefs of that foil with which nature has bleft them: climate here favours vegetation to fuch a degree as requires little toil in the hufbandman but that little is denied, fo that beyond oranges, bananas, pine-apples, cocoa nuts, yams and purflain, (all growing fpontaneoufly,) few vegetables are met with; nor are the natural beauties of the ifland inferior to its other advantages of plenty and fertility, the face of the country is very picturefque and pleafing, its fcenes are drawn by the bold ftrokes of nature's mafterly pencil : lofty mountains cloathed to their very fummits; deep and rugged vallies adorned by frequent cataracts and cafcades; woods, rocks and rivulets intermixed in "gay theatric pride" form the landfcape: groves are feen extending over the plains, to the very edge of the fea, formed principally by cocoa-nut trees, whofe long and naked ftems leave a clear uninterrupted paffage beneath, while their tufted and overfpreading tops form a thick fhade above, and keep off the fcorching rays of the fun; in these we pitch our tents and enjoy a short relief from the *ennui* of a tedious voyage.

In the interior part of the island surrounded by mountains of a prodigious height and about fifteen miles from this town is situated a sacred lake half a mile in circumference, the adjacent hills covered with lofty trees and the unfrequented solitude of the place seem more calculated to inspire religious awe in those who visit this sequestered spot, than any sanctity that is to be discovered in a parcel of wild ducks inhabiting it which are deified and worshipped by the original natives, who consult them as their oracles on all important affairs and sacrifice to them: being extremely averse to conduct strangers there, they stipulate that all guns shall be left at a place five miles from the lake; the worship paid to these birds ensures their safety and tranquillity, and rendering them of course perfectly tame they fearlesly approach any one who goes there: the Arabian part of the islanders hold this barbarous superstition in the utmost detestation, but dare not forbid the practice of it, so bigotted to it are the others.

This island produces no great variety of birds or beasts; amongst the former the Madagascar Bat is the most curious on account of its size and form, its dimensions between the extremities of
each

each wing when extended are near a yard and of its body from the tip of the nose to the tail about nine inches, the wings are of the same texture as those of the common bat, but the body is covered with a furr exactly of the colour and quality of that of a fox to which animal it bears likewise a perfect resemblance in its head, and for that reason some call it the flying fox; they abound on the coast of Africa and in the island of Madagascar, where they are much larger than here; they are said to be of a very voracious nature and to destroy fowls and other domestic animals.

The heat is very great at present and the thermometer near 90; our scorbutic men have found the benefit of shore and are tolerably recovered; all are embarked to-day and preparations made for our departure to morrow, when, if the wind permits, we shall be again launched into the dreary ocean and with good luck may expect to see the Indian shores in six weeks, a mere nothing of time to us who have passed six months at sea, but I dare say is more than you ever wish to spend on that joyless element. Adieu.

LETTER V.

Morebat Bay, Dec. 1, 1781.

DEAR FRIEND.

WE are, I believe, doomed to wander over the whole face of the ocean and never to arrive at our deſtin'd port; to moulder away in inactivity and loſe by ſickneſs thoſe lives, which it is true we owe to our country, but we ſhould wiſh for her ſake and our own to pay rather in the field than tamely on the ſea.

Our loſs has been very great ſince we left Joanna, an epidemical fever having raged in the fleet which has carried off a great number of officers and men; people will tell you that this has proceeded from a particular malignity in the air of Joanna; but I fancy it is no more than that particular malignity prevailing in all hot countries where there is much wood and where of courſe the night dews are very plentiful, theſe are always pernicious to men whoſe occupations and duty oblige them to be be expofed to their effect. One valley in particular proved very fatal to them that fixed their refidence in it; thofe natural beauties of which it boafted, formed by a thick grove of cocoa-nut trees through which a limpid ftream murmured and glided to the fea in gentle mæanders, ferved but as a decoy deftructive to fuch as were thereby enticed into its bofom; and that it was a more unhealthy fpot than any other muft be owing to its being more covered with trees, and by that means more fubject to the putrid and ftagnant vapour found fo baleful.

Phyficians who write on the difeafes of Europeans in hot climates recommend it to people who touch at places in thefe latitudes, for the purpofe of refrefhment, to fleep always on board of fhip, and it would have been more prudent in us to have conformed to their directions in that inftance, fince the ficknefs which has carried off fo many affected thofe principally who flept on fhore, amongft whom I happened unluckily to be, for tired with my long captivity on the fea, I could not refift the temptation of land, and lived entirely on the ifland, but have paid feverely for it by the lofs of my health which ever fince has been on the decline.

During the firft month after our leaving Joanna we received almoft every day the melancholy tidings

tidings of some friend's death, and in our visits from ship to ship hardly recognized others from their pale and emaciated appearance, beholding with sorrow

> " To infant weakness sunk the warrior's arm,
> " The lip pale-quivering and the beamless eye.
> " Heard nightly plung'd amid the sullen waves
> " The frequent corse: while on each other fix'd
> " In sad presage the blank assistants seem'd
> " Silent to ask, whom Fate would next demand."
>
> THOMSON.

At the same time that I lament this mortality which raged in our little army, allow me to animadvert on what in my opinion has been more than the noxious air of Joanna, a cause of the misfortune, namely the crowded and confined situation of our people on board of ship. The transports commonly made use of for the accommodation of troops are more calculated to destroy than preserve health, which can certainly be attributed to no other cause than the difficulty of procuring ships, for no pains or expence ought to be spared to promote so essential a point as the preservation of the men. Did not humanity dictate such a consideration, œconomy ought to point out the necessity of saving those lives which are replaced at so great an expence, greater than *that* would be of giving the troops better and more roomy

roomy transports; and by this means, saving half that perish at sea: but this should only be a secondary thought; the value of a British Soldier ought to be the first. In voyages of a moderate length, the health of the men may be better preserved on shipboard than on shore, provided they have room, good air, and wholesome provisions; care of officers may give every thing else; but their utmost efforts can never keep the men in health where those requisites are wanting. It has been our misfortune, though going on so long a voyage, to have only the same allowance of tonnage that those have, which are bound to America or the West Indies, viz. two ton per man, abundantly too small for them, what then must it be for us going to India? This mischief has been plainly pointed out by several ships that have been extremely sickly till near half their complements were buried, and after that, became as healthy: we might learn from this fatal experience, what quantity of tonnage would be proper for such a number of men. If therefore, we value the lives of our soldiers, and wish them to be landed compleat and fit for service in those countries to which they are sent, we ought to give them a better conveyance than at present, and take into the service, ships more proper for that purpose: the deck on which the men lay, ought to be pierced fore and aft; and by that means a constant current of air would keep it sweet and clean, an advantage not to be obtained in our present style of transports, whose lower decks are pestilential dungeons, and even on whose upper ones, from the number of men constantly there during the day-time, the air is putrid and unwholsome. Large ships are the fittest for trooptransports, for many reasons; but chiefly, because discipline and their duty, can there best be taught to the men, which, by amusing the mind and exercising the body, preserve both in health and vigor. If for the purpose of expedition, coppered ships should be made use of, great care must be taken that a quantity of water be let into them every day, and pumped out again, otherwise, as those ships are extremely tight, the bilge water will corrupt, and render the air putrid: nor should the men ever be suffered to tow their meat over-board, since by rubbing against the sides of the ship, it contracts some of the bad quality of the copper, and is very injurious.

But to return to our voyage: the first three weeks from Joanna, gave us the earnest of a speedy arrival at Bombay, a favourable breeze continually befriending us; but at the expiration of that time, resigned us to calms, currents, and contrary winds, which have been our portion ever since: during a whole month while the heat was excessive in about 10. north latitude, we experienced one continued calm; nor was that the worst that befell us,

for

for the currents drove us confiderably out of our courfe; and, when at length a breeze fprung up, it was directly contrary, and certified us of the fhifting of the monfoon, which in thefe feas takes place about the latter end of October: this is the name given to thofe periodical winds that blow in the Indian ocean fix months from N. E. or thereabouts, and the other fix months from the oppofite points: we contended for a long time with this contrary wind; but as we rather loft than gained way, and began to ftand in need of water and refrefhments, we bore away for this bay, and came in here November 27th; and it is much doubted whether the fleet, in which are many heavy and bad failing fhips, will be able to make good its paffage to India till March or April, when the foutherly moonfoon fets in.

Chance could hardly have directed us to a more unpleafant or miferable place than Morebat; the country here, does not refrefh the eye with a fingle vegetable production, but barren hills and fandy plains are the only objects to be feen; of fruits it yields none, and of cattle, only a few half-ftarved goats and bullocks, not larger than maftiff-dogs; the water we procure is little better than a diftillation of the fea water, which by oozing through the fand, loofes fome of its falt particles; and to get it, we are obliged to fink wells.

wells. Yet these blessings of life, such as I describe them, draw down upon the natives, the Budoos or wild Arabs, who inhabit the mountains: what then must *their* situation be, when they envy the people of Morebat, the little they possess? or where can the attachment to the *natale solum*, be more strongly shown than by these people who will fight to defend a country, one thinks it would be a happiness to be deprived of? From the frequent incursions which the Budoos make into this district, the inhabitants are kept on a perpetual *qui vive*; and from their constant state of warfare, have acquired a ferocity of look and manner, which makes them at least appear terrible; they have long ragged black hair, which they collect in a knot at the top of their heads; are naked, except a rug about their middle, and carry either a lance or match-lock gun; in marching to and from battle, they go in a rank, and before them dance some warriors, singing at the same time discordant airs, and clashing their shields and arms.

Abdallah Ben Homed the Noqueeb or Chief of Morebat, is now languishing with some wounds he received in battle, and lays stretched on a pallet in the corner of a gloomy cellar, which is his *salle d'audience*, where we are introduced to him, and seat ourselves on the ground

COAST OF ARABIA FELIX, &c. 37

ground to take coffee with him and his generals, while the Hookah passes round; this is a pipe of a singular and complicated construction, through which tobacco is smoked: out of a small vessel of a globular form, and nearly full of water, issue two tubes, one perpendicularly, on which is placed the tobacco; the other, obliquely from the side of the vessel, and to that the person who smokes, applies his mouth; the smoke by this means being drawn through water, is cooled in its passage, and rendered more grateful: one takes a whiff, draws up a large quantity of smoke, puffs it out of his nose and mouth in an immense cloud, and passes the hookah to his neighbour; and thus it goes round the whole circle. The hookah is known and used throughout the East; but in those parts of it where the refinements of life prevail more than at Morebat, every one has his hookah sacred to himself; and it is frequently an implement of a very costly nature, being of silver, and set with precious stones: in the better kind, that tube which is applied to the mouth is very long and pliant; and for that reason is termed the snake: people who use it in a luxurious manner, fill the vessel through which the smoke is drawn with rose water, and it thereby receives some of the fragrant quality of that fluid.

The interior part of the country is occupied by Budoos, jackalls and wild dogs; all which descend

scend to prey on the sandy plains of Morebat. Would you think, that of all countries, this unhappy place should be situated on the coast of happy Arabia? If one may judge of it from the specimen here exhibited, no term was ever more misapplied, where the country is destitute of every vegetable production, the natives of every rational enjoyment.

Large fleets of Arabian vessels are daily passing full of pilgrims going to Mecca, and merchandise brought from Muscat, Bussora, and other places on the coast, being bound for Mocha and Juddah in the Red Sea; the passage to the former place from hence, is but about ten days; and the easy transition to Europe by that route, will I believe, induce me to seek cooler climes for the recovery of my health, to which these torrid ones are so unfriendly: if I meet with an Arabian vessel that can accommodate me tolerably well for the short distance to Mocha, the India Company's agent will put me in the proper channel to get up the Red Sea, or I may possibly find an European ship to convey me to Suez; from thence across the Isthmus of that name to Alexandria, is not above a six day's journey, and I shall then be on the borders of the Mediterranean sea, with daily opportunities of passing into Italy, or some part of Europe.

The

The hopes of regaining so valuable a possession as health, can alone make me form this wish, as I shall give up my Indian expedition with the greatest reluctance; but as I retire from the sun, I flatter myself, I shall receive daily benefit; and that by the time I arrive in England, I shall be fit for a campaign in the temperate zone. Adieu.

LETTER

LETTER VI.

Mocha, Dec. 30, 1781.

DEAR FRIEND.

YOU will perceive by the date of this, that I have put into execution the defign, of which I gave fome hints in my laſt, and am thus far in my way to Europe.

I embarked about three weeks ago in an Arabian veſſel that came into Morebat Bay for water, and was bound hither: my accommodations on board it, were not magnificent, but I had every thing that common wants required, and had an opportunity of learning of what difadvantage it is on many occafions to have too many of them, it is true,

> They prove a fource of pleafure when fupply'd.
> GOLDSMITH.

but *vice versâ* of pain when unprovided for. I found myfelf rather uncomfortable at firſt on that account,

account, not being able to drink my tea, or make my meals quite so much at my ease as I was used to do; but seeing my copper-coloured fellow travellers happy with a little rice and water, and not distressed for want of tables, chairs and napkins, I adopted their customs more consonant to nature than my own, and soon reasoned myself into good humour, both with my situation and fare, and having a tolerable cabbin, was not in danger of suffering from the sun by day, or the dews by night. The Noquedah or master of the vessel, by name Hamet Ali, was a venerable old man, with a long white beard, and had a benignity of countenance that prepossessed me in his favour; his people likewise seemed to be good honest fellows, and I readily embarked on board his vessel, notwithstanding, some of my friends thought it rather an hazardous step, but I took care not to throw the temptation of booty in their way, taking with me, scarce any thing but my bedding and provisions, and giving them credit for so much liberality of sentiment as not to suspect any harm, because I was not of their colour, or did not, like them, believe Mahomet to be the true prophet. However, I endeavoured to cultivate their good will as much as possible; and on first going on board, sat down with the Noquedah and his officers to supper, the floor being both our table and chairs, on which we seated ourselves in a circle, with a large bowl of rice in the middle, and some fish and dates before each person: here I likewise found that knives and forks were useless instruments in eating, and that nature had accommodated us with what answered the same purpose: we plunged our hands into the bowl, rolled up an handful of rice into a ball, and conveyed it to our mouths in that form: our repast was short, and to that succeeded coffee and washing, and on their parts prayer, in which they were very frequent and fervent, always going through the motions of it together by signal from a man advanced before them, and every evening they chaunted forth Alla Alla, and the praises of Mahomet for an hour or two after sun-set.

Our vessel was one of the largest of this kind, and had thirty hands on board: all those craft are built very sharp at the head, and sail extremely fast, although they carry but one sail; they are built of thin planks, sown or rather laced together with cord; their ropes are made of Kiar the filament which covers the cocoa-nut shell, and their sails of cotton: in our passage we steered from headland to headland, and were never far from land, which along the whole extent of the coast, appeared barren and rugged; as they take only three or four days water on board at a time, we were frequently obliged to put in at different places for a supply, which made our passage rather tedious, and what might have been done in eight days was, owing to

that

that circumstance, protracted to a fortnight, when we arrived here.

This city appears extremely beautiful as you approach it, being well built, and standing close to the water's edge; the houses are very lofty, and are, as well as the walls, forts, &c. covered with a chinam or stucco, that gives a dazzling whiteness to them: the harbour is semicircular, and formed by two arms which run out into the sea to equal lengths, having a fort at each extremity. The circuit of the wall is two miles: there are several handsome mosques in the city; but that with the tower built in honour of Shadeli, who founded the town, and brought the coffee plant into the neighbourhood, is the principal one. The English, French and Dutch have factories here; the house of the former is a very large and handsome building, in which I am comfortably lodged, and have already received benefit from the salubrity of the air, and other refreshments which I meet with. The climate is now temperate and pleasant, compared with what I have lately experienced, though the thermometer is generally up at 80. in the middle of the day, and at 77. in the mornings and evenings; there are no springs of fresh water in the town, but some of a very good quality within a quarter of a mile amongst the groves of date trees: provisions, fruits and vegetables are in great abundance.

Trade has much declined here of late years, since Europe has been supplied with coffee from the West-Indies, which article is the staple commodity of this country; it grows at a place called Betelfaqui, sixty miles from hence, and is brought here on camels: that patient and docile animal, in these eastern countries, shares with man in his toil, and transports his merchandise from place to place; he kneels down at the command of his master to receive his load, and carries it with a slow and steady pace across dry and barren deserts, supporting thirst for several days together; nor is this animal useful only for the purposes of carrying a rider or his burden, but likewise supplies man both with food and raiment.

The finest breed of Arabian horses is in this country, and has furnished us with those we make use of for the turf; they are here chiefly articles of luxury, used only in war, or for parade: the governor has a large stud opposite to the house where I live, which affords me much pleasure as I pay them frequent visits; they are small, but finely shaped, and extremely active; of this I had an opportunity of judging yesterday when the cavalry had a field-day in the great square, which, from the mode of exercise, called to my mind the idea of our antient tilts and tournaments: the lists were surrounded by a great number of spectators, and within were

drawn

drawn up fifty horsemen; they first moved in a body, and performed several charges with great rapidity, then dispersed, some took antagonists, and practised with them a mock fight with lances of ten or twelve yards in length, which they all carried; others went singly through their exercise with that weapon, and the motions of attack and defence; their horses were sumptuously caparisoned, being adorned with gold and silver trappings, bells hung round their necks, and rich housings; the riders were in handsome Turkish dresses, with white turbans, and the whole formed to me a new and pleasing spectacle. There is a very martial spirit amongst the Arabians in general; and the constant state of warfare they are in with the Budoos, tends much to keep it up: these roving banditti, who are spread over the whole country, occasionally form themselves into numerous bodies for the purpose of plunder; and often by their depredations, bring down upon themselves the Sovereign of the country at the head of his army, who frequently finds great difficulty in driving them away.

The kingdom of Sunnaa, in which stands this city, is situated in the finest part of Arabia, and that which, from its fertility, best deserves the epithet we annex to it; the Arabians term this district Yemen: the Imaum or king of Sunnaa, resides at the metropolis of that name in the interior

rior part of the country, ten days journey from hence, (a day's journey being twenty-five miles;) the two firſt days you paſs through the ſame flat and ſandy plain as that which ſurrounds this place; but beyond that, the country is fertile, and well cultivated, being diverſified with hill and dale: the town of Sunnaa ſtands amongſt mountains, and always enjoys a temperate climate. The circuit of the kingdom, they ſay, is ſix hundred miles: the Imaum has a large army in pay: he lives in great ſtate at his capital, has a numerous ſtud of very fine horſes, and his ſeraglio is compoſed of one hundred and fifty women: in this bleſſing of life, people may here indulge themſelves to what extent they pleaſe, there being no limitation to the number of concubines, though only four wives are allowed; the ſeraglios are therefore commonly in proportion to the wealth of the maſter, their concubines being ſlaves whom they purchaſe: their idea of beauty, as may eaſily be ſuppoſed, differs as much from our's as their colour; the more jetty black the complexion of the female, the more is ſhe admired; flat noſes and thick lips, are conſidered handſome; and therefore, the women of Abyſſina, which country is oppoſite to this coaſt, having thoſe perfections in the higheſt degree, fetch the greateſt price in the market; numbers of them are brought here, and ſent to the other parts of Arabia every year for ſale. Where a man has only a few women, they all

COAST OF ARABIA FELIX, &c. 47

all live together in the same house, within which, they are kept close prisoners, the jealousy of the master hardly ever allowing them to stir abroad, but never on any account to be seen by or speak to another man.

The Gentoos are very numerous in this city; these are a particular sect of men that are scatter'd throughout the East, and are no less simple in their life and manners than singular in their doctrine: the founder of them was Brama who gave them their creed; they are distributed into what we term *castes* or communities of men who practise the same occupation and keep themselves distinct from each other, they hold it the greatest of crimes to drink out of the same vessel with one of another *caste* or religion, never eat of any animal, or kill even a fly, this lenity is founded on their belief in the *metempsychosis* which also induces them to feed all kinds of animals, not knowing but that the souls of some of their friends may have taken up their abode in the bodies of them, so that the dogs, cats, cows, pigeons, fowls, &c. subsist mostly by the charity of the Gentoos, the owners of them thinking it unnecessary to be at the expence of feeding them when these good gentlemen are taught by their religion to take so much care of them.

Chescron

Chefcron Hadjee the English Agent is of that tribe, he has large *converfazionis* every afternoon, compofed of his brother Banians, (the denomination given to fuch as are of the mercantile *cafte*) who fit round the room on cufhions and take coffee with him, they are of a lighter colour than any other people here, and fome of them might in looks pafs for fallow Europeans, they drefs in a long clofe-bodied muflin gown and a red turban made up into a form fomething like a woman's bonnet; they cherifh one fingle lock on the crown of the head, fhaving all the reft, and generally have a red wafer ftuck in the middle of their forehead, which is a religious badge placed there by the priefts.

I was witnefs yefterday to a curious ceremony, called in the Eaft *champooing*; coming accidentally into the apartment where my friend Chefcron, who is a little deformed dropfical old man, generally lays reclined on cufhions, I beheld him ftretched out quite naked on the floor, and proftrate on his face, while his attendants were rubbing him; I was at firft apprehenfive, that the old fellow had fallen down in a fit, and thought they were trying to bring him to life again; they laid hold of his flefh in different parts, pinching and clawing him with great violence; I approached him with fome fear; when hearing me fpeak, he turned up his brown face with a
smile

smile, by which I found that all was right with him, and to my surprize heard, that this operation was looked on as salutary, and extremely pleasant; it must without doubt promote a circulation of the blood, and supplenefs of the joints, every one of which they pull and pinch, but I hardly think we shall ever borrow this luxury from the East.

There are many rich merchants here, but as their wealth increafes, the sovereign makes a demand for his share, which is as much as he chufes to ask for: when his wants are preffing, he sends orders to the governor to demand a free gift of so many dollars from the merchants, which they freely give, becaufe they dare not refufe: the governor affeffes them according to his own pleafure, dividing the sum to be raifed between Banians and Muffulmen.

In travelling through different countries, the first idea that fuggefts itfelf is, whether the laws and customs which prevail, are fuch as tend to make the people happy; and in forming this eftimation, we are but too apt to meafure their feelings by our own, which is in fact to confider whether we should ourselves be happy in them, arguing on this principle, we muft of courfe draw our comparifon much to the difadvantage of that country, where the violation of property is fo cuftomary as it is here; and the intercourfe with the *beau fexe* is founded on tyranny and compulfion,

instead

instead of that delicacy and sympathy of sentiment which forms those attachments with us. But to weigh the matter fairly, we should pronounce, that if an Englishman would be miserable in Arabia Felix, an Arabian would be no less so in England; the force of custom, climate and complexion, which makes men equally happy in different quarters of the globe, will not allow them to be transplanted more than the fruits of the country, which can only flourish in their proper soils. I believe the *fonds* of happiness are pretty nearly the same throughout the world, and that nature has in all places adapted the country and the natives of it to each other. Adieu.

LETTER

LETTER VII.

Juddah, March 6, 1782.

DEAR FRIEND.

I Know not whether the satisfaction I had, on arriving at this place or that which I shall receive on quitting it, will be the greatest: the former proceeded from its being the period of a tedious passage from Mocha, the latter will arise from the pleasure one must naturally feel at leaving a place that has not the means of affording any.

I embarked at Mocha in a trankey of the same kind as that which conveyed me from Morebat; and sailing in the evening with a fresh breeze and rough sea, which I thought would swallow up my little vessel, reached Hodeida the next afternoon: that place is in the kingdom of Sunnaa; and being nearer to Betelfaqui than Mocha, ships off much more coffee for Juddah: the master of the vessel detained me here two days greatly against my own will and his professions before we set off; he took at this place a pilot, as all the coasting vessels do; and being again embarked, we sailed at midnight, and had a much higher sea than we experienced between Mocha and Hodeida; the swell was so great, that I doubted much whether our cockle shell would be able to live in it; we were tossed about in a very alarming manner for twelve hours, and then arrived and anchored off the small island of Camaran, famous only for its good water.

We sailed early the next morning; the breeze was at first fair, but did not long continue so, and almost ever after, during our passage, was contrary, and by that means it was protracted to eight and twenty days, though frequently performed in eight or ten. Our course lay along shore betwixt the main land and a chain of little islands, with which, as likewise with rocks and shoals the sea abounds in this part; and for that reason it is the practice with all these vessels to anchor every evening: we generally brought up close to the shore, and the land breeze springing up about midnight, wafted to us the perfumes of Arabia, with which it was strongly impregnated and very fragrant; the latter part of it, carried us off in the morning, and continued till eight, when it generally fell calm for two or three hours, and after that the northerly wind set in,

often

often obliging us to anchor under the lee of the land by noon: it happened that one morning when we had been driven by ſtreſs of weather into a ſmall bay called Birk Bay, the country around it being inhabited by the Budoos, the Noquedah ſent his people on ſhore to get water, for which it is always cuſtomary to pay: The Budoos were as the people thought, rather too exorbitant in their demands; and not chuſing to comply with them, returned to make their report to their maſter; on hearing it, rage immediately ſeized him, and determined to have the water on his own terms, or periſh in the attempt, he buckled on his armour, and attended by his myrmidons, carrying their match-lock guns and lances, being twenty in number, they rowed to the land: my Arabian ſervant, who went on ſhore with the firſt party, and ſaw that the Budoos were diſpoſed for fighting, told me that I ſhould certainly ſee a battle; I accordingly looked on very anxiouſly, hoping that the fortune of the day would be on the ſide of my friends, but heaven ordained it otherwiſe; for after a parley of about a quarter of an hour, with which the Budoos amuſed them till near an hundred were aſſembled, they proceeded to the attack and routed the ſailors, who made a precipitate retreat, the Noquedah and two having fallen in the action, and ſeveral being wounded; they contrived however to bring off their dead; and the group around the body of the Noquedah

was

was truly moving; the grief expressed by all, testified the regard they bore him, but in none was so strongly marked as in the furrowed face of an old slave, who looked on with silent anguish while a tear trickled down his cheek. The weather obliged us to pass that and the following day in the disagreeable neighbourhood of our enemies; and my Arabian servant Mahommed, in whose composition fear was a principal ingredient, took great pains to represent to me how practicable a thing it would be for the Budoos to cut us off in the night, since they would not have above a stone's throw to swim; and being so numerous, might easily board the trankey when every body was asleep; I assented very readily to what he said, and strongly recommending to him to keep a good look-out, doubted not but that his vigilance would render my repose secure.

Throughout this affair I could not but admire the spirit of my fellow travellers, altho' overpowered by numbers, they had unfortunately lost the day; and the generous sorrow expressed by them on the death of their leader, gave me a good opinion of their humanity and feelings: but an act of savage cruelty they committed three days after, entirely removed it.

One of the sailors died of his wounds, and at two o'clock they anchored near the land, and went on shore to bury him; three Budoos of a
different

COAST OF ARABIA FELIX, &c.   55

different tribe from those they had fought with, came down to the beach out of curiosity, and stood by as spectators of the ceremony, which being ended, the sailors, who were twelve in number, turned to these poor innocent fellows, told them that the man whom they had buried, was killed by some Budoos, and in revenge sacrificed these people to his *manes*, stabbing and mangling them in an horrid manner; they returned to the vessel exulting, and thinking they had performed a gallant action, seemed as they told their tale to demand from every one a smile of approbation, but not being able to give them one, I asked Mahommed, who joined in the general joy, how such an action could please him; he replied, that they had done very right, for their book ordered them always to kill an equal number of the same kind of people as had killed any of theirs: as a punishment to him for these *tenets*, I was not sorry that he had again a night of fear and watching; for towards dusk we discovered a large body of Budoos on the shore; this put him on thorns, and the idea of being cut off, did not (I believe) suffer him to get a wink of sleep all night. We left this bloody coast on the morning following, and stopping at a place called Confidah to get water, meeting with strong gales from north, which obliged us to remain at anchor for days together, but without any more adventures or blood-shed, we arrived here.

The

Tired with being cooped up so long in a small vessel, and anxious to pursue my route, I landed at this place with the hopes of leaving it in a day or two, and have been detained near six weeks, waiting for the sailing of the annual Suez fleet, recommended to me as the most eligible, or indeed the only safe mode of going thither.

When I say of Juddah, that it is *terra senza frutti & popolo senza Fede*, I believe I give you a pretty just description of it; but to enter into a more minute one, I must inform you that it is an old and ill-built town, surrounded by a broken and ruinous wall, having no fort, nor any guns mounted; it is situated nearly mid-way betwixt Mocha and Suez, on the eastern coast of the Red Sea, and is a place of the greatest trade on it: the commerce between Arabia and Europe here meets, and is interchanged; the former sending her gums, drugs, coffee, &c. which are brought in small vessels from the whole extent of the coast, as far as Bussora in the Persian Gulf, and from Europe come cloths, iron, furs and other articles, by way of Cairo: the revenue arising from the duties on these is shared by the Grand Signor and Xerif of Mecca, to whom this place jointly belongs: it was formerly tributary to the Grand Signor only; but the latter, whose dominions surround it, seized on it; the affair however being compromised between them, they now share the profits of the port:

port; the former sends annually a Pacha to support his pretensions, and collect the revenue; the latter deputes a governor who is termed the Vizir Xerif, and has the chief power and authority here: the man who at present in that capacity dispenses law and justice, is an Abyssinian eunuch, and was a slave in the late Xerif's family.

The people here are not quite so black as at Mocha, having a yellowish tinge in their complexions: their way of living is much the same as there; they sit crofs-legged on the ground at their meals, wash, pray, drink coffee, and smoke hookah five times in the day. There are several coffee-houses which are always full; the common people there drink their dish of coffee together as our's would their pot of beer at an alehouse. The women seem to have rather more liberty than at Mocha, as I see many of them walking about the streets; but the appearance they make is so extraordinary, that at first I was doubtful in what *genus* to class them; they wear loose cloth trowsers and yellow Hussar boots, have veils of white linen over their faces, reaching almost to the ground, with only two small slits for the eyes, and wrap themselves in a large loose plaid of coarse cloth; they have a variety of gold and silver trinkets round their arms and legs, and wear necklaces of small pieces of money strung; all these make a jingle like bells as they walk;

through

through one of their nostrils they wear a ring with a flat plate on it like a coat button and dye their hands red with an herb that grows in the country; they are as fond of smoaking hookah as the men; and when they visit, always take it along with them.

Being near the fountain-head of their faith, the people here are great bigots to their religion, and of course inveterate enemies to the christians; any stranger of that class is sure of being insulted in the streets, unless he has a guard with him; they are not allowed to go out of the gate leading to Mecca; and in their dress, must be careful to avoid green or white, two colours sacred to Mussulmen; and even of these, such only as are descended from Mahomet, may wear the green turban; nor are we thought by them to be worthy the honor of mounting an horse; for they say as our prophet contented himself with riding an ass, his followers have no right to be better mounted; but as the jack-ass is an animal whose paces I don't much admire, I take my exercise on foot, and can only walk for a short way by the sea side; though as the country around is all a desert, I do not regret that I cannot penetrate into it; the only circumstance from which I have received any satisfaction during my stay here is, the temperature of the air, which with sea bathing, has agreed very well with my northern constitution:

COAST OF ARABIA FELIX, &c. 59

tion: the thermometer having generally been below 70.

About a quarter of a mile north of the town is a white building called Eve's sepulchre; and they tell you that she was certainly buried there, and that her grave is twenty feet in length, which they determine to have been the standard height of mankind at that early period of the world; the two Arabick words *oumana boua*, signifying Eve the mother of all are inscribed on the building; they go every Sabbath to pray there, but will not suffer a christian to visit it. The two most valuable productions of this country are balm of Gilead and Senna, the former is extracted from a tree which grows amongst the mountains, the latter is a shrub found near Mecca.

Our merchants in India used to send annually ships from Bengal and other parts to Juddah, but the arbitrary impositions laid on the goods and the frauds they experienced from the people, has made them entirely discontinue this commerce: a most glaring instance of villany in the Prince of the country, and his Lord Lieutenant of Juddah stands foremost on the latter list; they jointly bought the cargo of an English ship worth near £.50,000, took the goods, and engaged to pay the money in a few days; but the Supercargo after repeated applications, was obliged to return to India, having only the Xerif's bill, payable the following summer; accordingly he returned, was very pressing for the money, but met with no better success than before, and only received a fresh bill, with positive assurances that he should be paid the following year; it happened that before his return, both the Xerif and his Vizir were dead, and when he applied for payment of the bill to the reigning Xerif, who was son to the former, he flatly refused to pay a farthing, saying, that as the debt was incurred by his father, his father only was answerable for it, that it was true he was dead, but the body was at his service, and if it would be any satisfaction to the creditors, he was very welcome to carry it to Bengal with him.

A place, where the natural advantages are so few and the moral defects so great, cannot you may suppose, be a pleasing one to spend much time at; I promise you I am impatient to quit it, and turn my face northward. Adieu.

LETTER

LETTER VIII.

Suez, April 25, 1782.

`DEAR FRIEND.

SHOULD I tell you that I arrived here yesterday after a passage of six weeks from Juddah, without entering into a detail of the manner in which I performed that voyage, I should do injustice to the Turkish mode of navigation on the Red Sea, and pay but a bad compliment to the Suez fleet whose performances ought not to be passed over in silence.

The construction and management of the vessels are equally singular and I fear any description will fall infinitely short of the originals; they were I believe, designed by those who built them to bear some resemblance to ships, but having very few of the properties of those machines proceed on a principle totally different
from

from any I before beheld; that *primum mobile* to which ships of other countries are indebted for their voyages is here of little use and calms are more favorable than wind to forward their progress, for unless the latter comes in a very small quantity they rarely chuse to expose their sails to it and herein seem equally averse to a fair as to a contrary wind, remaining at anchor till it subsides into a calm, their busy scene then commences, the anchor is weighed and the vessel put in motion by means of the boat with about twenty oars in it, towing till a breeze springs up, when this begins to be more than what our seamen call a light air they hurry to the shore and let go their anchor, and for this purpose always chuse a birth the most environed by rocks and shoals, never thinking themselves secure but when in the midst of danger; their common time of anchoring, was about two o'clock in the afternoon for about that time the breeze generally freshened, and in proportion as that encreases they put out anchors till they have six in the water and two or three hawsers besides to tie them to the surrounding rocks: in this situation did we frequently remain for days together; but in what they called good weather we had not above two anchors out and if it fell calm after sun set they ventured to get one of them up that they might be ready for the land breeze in the morning, which generally

sprung

sprung up at two o'clock and blew till nine or ten, and as it hardly made a curl on the water suited our mariners exactly, they always got under way with it as soon as it was light and sometimes before; I believe without these landbreezes, we should never have arrived at Suez, a circumstance that very frequently happens to many vessels of this annual fleet, for if they do not make good their passage before the latter end of May, the northerly winds blow so constantly as to render it impossible, for vessels that cannot work to windward, to get up the narrow channel from Tor to Suez.

As we remained then every afternoon at anchor near the shore, nor ever ventured far from it when under way; you may suppose that, in the course of my voyage, I had sufficient opportunity to make my observations both on the Red Sea famous in the sacred history, and likewise on the coast of Arabia which was perpetually before my eyes; the latter being Arabia Deserta, is literally what its name implies; the former presented no appearance that justifies the term given to it proceeding as some authors say from a reddish tinge on the waters, but no such did I ever take notice of: our climate was always clear and serene and became much more temperate as we moved northward, indeed the wind
chiefly

chiefly blowing from that quarter made the air cool: during the latter part of our paffage, it has blown very frefh at times, and obliged us once to remain at anchor eight days together in the fame place: our fleet has fuffered very much thereby; and we are laying here at prefent in company with four other veffels, and are the only ones that have as yet got up: intelligence over land informs us of the lofs of four, driven from their anchors in the blowing weather, and wrecked; and that two others anchored near the fhore, were in the night boarded and plundered by the Budoos; one was wrecked a day or two after we left Juddah, fo that five of them being loft, and two plundered, near one third of the fleet is difpofed of that way; five are at Suez, and the reft have not been heard of: you may be fure that I think myfelf fortunate in having arrived here amongft the firft, and efcaped all the perils of this curious voyage of about two hundred leagues; nor am I fo much furprifed that we have been near fifty days in performing it, as that, confidering their mode of manœuvring, we fhould be able to perform it at all. But to give you a more exact idea thereof, I will tranfcribe for your perufal the journal I kept on board the Mahaboube, bound from Juddah to the port of Suez. The daily height of the thermometer I have not fet down for any particular hour, but have taken it

always

always at the higheft point it was at in the courfe of the day.

March 10. Embarked this afternoon on board the Mahaboube, a veffel of about five hundred tons burthen, laden with coffee and pilgrims returning from the Hadge, (the annual feftival of the Muffulmen held at Mecca;) thefe lay intermingled on the deck; each perfon has a fmall fpace allotted to him where he fleeps, cooks his victuals, &c. The great cabbin and round-houfe are divided into fmall births for paffengers. This veffel is built very high at the poop, and fquare at the bows; it is fteered by a fingular contrivance acrofs the deck; between the mizen and the main maft is placed a large beam, which projects near twenty feet from the fhip's fides; to each end of this beam is fixed a fmall one twelve feet long, the centre thereof being tied to the end of the great beam, but fo as to allow it to move backwards and forwards: from one end of this fmall beam paffes a rope to the rudder, and from the other end a rope to the helmfman, who fits at the aftermoft part of the poop and fteers.

11. Dropped down to the mouth of the channel, which is very narrow and difficult; anchored there at noon. In making fail, they hoift up the yards with the fails loofe; the lower yards being laid acrofs the decks while at anchor, the upper ones

ones refting on the tops. The pilot is ftationed on the bowfprit from whence he gives directions to the helmfman. The fails are of ftriped and figured cotton. The fhips are painted dark brown, with figures and ornaments in white and red.

12. The fleet compofed of twenty-five fail of different forms and fizes, weighed at fix A. M. and proceeded in company: they mean to keep together till they have paffed Yambo, which has lately been taken from the Xerif of Mecca by the Budoos, who have large boats, and it is thought, mean to attack the fleet, or at leaft any ftraggling fhips they meet with. Light air from fouth. Anchored at four P. M. Thermometer 82. Diftance gone about twenty miles.

13. Weighed at five A. M. Light air from weft fouth weft. Anchored at four P. M. Diftance twenty miles. Thermometer 83.

14. Weighed at four A. M. with the land breeze. Calm at ten A. M. Towed till 12. Sea-breeze then fet in, and we anchored at two P. M. Diftance fixteen miles. Thermometer 85.

15. Weighed at four A. M. with the land breeze. Calm at nine. Towed moft part of the day, and anchored at four P. M. Diftance fixteen miles. Thermometer 88.

16. At

16. At anchor, wind north-weft. Thermometer 80.

17. Sailed at seven A. M. with a land breeze. Calm at eleven. Light air from north weft at noon. Anchored at four P. M. Diftance fifteen miles.

18. Sailed at fix A. M. with a light air. Calm at nine. Towed till noon, when breeze from north weft fprung up, and we anchored at two P. M. Diftance 15 miles. Thermometer 80.

19. Sailed at four A. M. with the land breeze. Calm at eleven. Towed till noon, when a light air from north weft fprung up. Anchored at five P. M. Diftance twenty miles. Thermometer 82.

20. Sailed at fix. A. M. Anchored at two P. M. Wind weft. Diftance twenty miles. Thermometer 83.

21. Sailed at four A. M. anchored at two P. M. off Yambo, in company with the fleet, diftant about a mile from the town: it is a good looking place, has feveral mofques and a caftle.

22. At anchor. Wind blowing frefh from north weft. Thermometer 79. Our boats pafs unmolefted

lested backwards and forwards, between the ships and the town for water and provisions.

23. At anchor. Wind north west. Thermometer 79.

24. At anchor. Wind north west. Thermometer 80.

25. Sailed at sun-rise. Anchored at three P. M. Wind west south west. Thermometer $85\frac{1}{4}$.

26. Sailed early with the land-breeze. Calm at nine A. M. Towed till noon. Sea breeze set in, anchored at three P. M. Thermometer 86.

27. Sailed at five A. M. Anchored at three P. M. off Gebel Hassani, a small island, being abreast of Haura on the main land. Thermometer $84\frac{1}{2}$.

28. Sailed with the land breeze at five A. M. Calm at ten. North wind set in at noon. Anchored at four P. M. Thermometer 84. A thunder storm at night.

29. Sailed at six A. M. Anchored at four P. M. Thermometer 79.

30. Sailed

30. Sailed at fix A. M. Anchored at five P. M. Light air weft. Thermometer 83.

31. Sailed at feven A. M. Paffed through a narrow channel of about a mile in length, and not more than twice the breadth of the fhip, with rocks and fands on each fide: after the fhips had paffed through it, they fired guns for joy, it being confidered the moft dangerous part of the voyage.

April 1. Sailed at feven A. M. Anchored at noon. Wind north weft. Thermometer 76.

2. Sailed at fix A. M. Anchored at four P. M. having paffed Shek Bermak, a fmall ifland at the extremity of a chain of fands and iflands that extend from Gebel Haffani thither. Thermometer 77.

3. Sailed at four A. M. and it being calm in the evening, we ftood on towing moft part of the night. Thermometer 85.

4. Calm till ten A. M. Wind fet in from north, anchored at eleven A. M. Thermometer 81.

5. Sailed at three A. M. Anchored at three P. M. Light air from weft. Thermometer 83.

6. Sailed

6. Sailed with the land breeze at one A. M. Anchored at three P. M. Thermometer 80.

7. Sailed at fix A. M. Anchored at five P. M. near Iflam. Several Arabs and camels came down to the beach, and fome people went from hence by land to Cairo, a journey of fourteen days.

8. Sailed with the land breeze at one A. M. Paffed Moilah at five P. M. and the wind being fair and moderate, continued our courfe during the night, ftanding over for Raz Mahommed: the wind fhifted at midnight to north, and drove us up into the Eaftern Fork of the fea almoft as far as Acaba. Thermometer 85.

9. Wind contrary, made little way and anchored at three P. M. Thermometer 80.

10. Sailed at feven A. M. Light air at north weft. Anchored at fix P. M. Thermometer 84.

11. Sailed at fix A. M. Paffed the iflands Tyran and Senaffre. Anchored at two P. M. in a fmall bay called Sharm. Two or three hundred Arabs came down to the beach on camels. The captain of our fhip fent his boat for the Scheik, and gave him prefents of coffee, &c. Our people feemed to have fome apprehenfions from thefe

Arabs,

Arabs, loading their arms, and keeping watch all night. Thermometer 85.

12. Sailed at two A. M. with a fair wind, paffed Raz Mahommed at five A. M. which event they celebrated by firing guns. Paffed the ifle of Sheduan at feven A. M. and Tor, at one P. M. foon after came in fight of Mount Sinai and Horeb; the former is here called Taurofina: on it is a convent of Greek catholicks, to which many chriftians make pilgrimages; to enter it, you muft be hoifted in a bafket up a very high precipice on which it ftands. Thermometer 84. we ftood on during the night.

13. At one A. M. a breeze from north fet in, at day light we made for the fhore, and anchored clofe to it. Thermometer 83.

14. At anchor. Wind blowing frefh from north. Thermometer at fun-rife 66.

15. At anchor, it blowing frefh. Thermometer at fun-rife 62½. Two veffels which were anchored near us, drove afhore in the night, and went to pieces; the people were with difficulty faved, fome of which we took on board.

16. At anchor, it blowing frefh. Thermometer at fun-rife 67.

17. At

17. At anchor. Wind north. Thermometer 75, at two P. M.

18. At anchor. Wind north. Thermometer at fun-rife 65, at two P. M. 80. Arabs and camels are daily paffing along the fhore. Some people from a fhip (anchored near us) fet off to-day by land to Suez, a journey of five days on camels.

19. At anchor. Wind north. Thermometer at fun-rife 66; at two P. M. 74.

20. At anchor. Wind north. Thermometer at fun-rife 66; at two P. M. 74.

21. Sailed at fix A. M. with a fair wind, and at two P. M. paffed Burkit Pharoon, fignifying Pharaoh's whirlpool. This they determine to be that part of the Red Sea which Mofes and the children of Ifrael croffed, as related in the bible, when purfued by Pharaoh, who they fay was drowned in that very fpot where this eddy is. Our people here killed a fheep, cut off it's head, which they fmoked with incenfe, and threw it into the fea, praying at the fame time. The high land on the Arabian fhore is called the Hummum, from a fpring of boiling water on it. This place is half way between Tor and Suez. The wind continuing fair and moderate, we ftood on till eleven

eleven P. M. when it shifted to west, and we anchored.

22. At anchor. Wind north. Thermometer at sun-rise 64. at two P. M. 76.

23. Sailed at seven A. M. Anchored at eight P. M. Thermometer at two P. M. 75. Suez in sight from the mast-head at sun-set.

24. Sailed at sun-rise. Anchored off Suez at four P. M. Thermometer 70.

Suez, which was the Arsinoe of the antients, is situated at the top of the Red Sea; it stands surrounded by the Desert, and is a shabby ill-built place: the ships anchor a league from the town, to which the channel that leads is very narrow, and has only nine or ten feet depth of water; for which reason, the large ships that are built here, must be towed down to the road without masts, guns, or any thing in them; there are eight of them laying here which have not been to Juddah this year; one of them is at least twelve hundred tons burthen, being as lofty as an hundred-gun-ship, though not longer than a frigate; so that you may judge of the good proportions they observe in the construction of their ships: the timber of which they are all built, is brought from Syria by water to Cairo, and from thence on camels,

mels. This fleet sails for Juddah every year before the Hadge, stays there two or three months, and returns loaded with coffee: this is so material an article in the diet of a Mussulman, that the prayers and wishes of them all are offered up for its safety; and I believe next to the loss of their country, the loss of their coffee would be most severely felt by them: the greatest part of it is sent to Constantinople, and other parts of Turkey, but a small quantity going to France and Italy.

Suez is so wretched a place, that though, as you may suppose, I am heartily tired of my Turkish ship, yet sooner than stay on shore, I prefer waiting on board it till the Caravan sets out for Cairo, which will be in two or three days. I shall not be a little pleased when this passage of the Desert is over, to which I look forward with a kind of dread from the heat and fatigue likely to attend it, the season being advanced far beyond my expectations when I first turned my face towards Europe; but my health is much mended of late, and I flatter myself will be equal to the fatigue of the journey; besides when I consider that it will be only of three days continuance, and all the remainder of my way will be smooth and easy, I shall bear the inconvenience more patiently. Adieu.

LETTER

LETTER IX.

Cairo, May 1, 1782.

DEAR FRIEND.

I ARRIVED at this place early yesterday morning after a most disagreeable journey acrofs the Defert, but fortunately a fhorter one than ufual, having performed it in a day and an half.

When I tell you that I came with a Caravan from Suez, I fhould likewife tell you, that a Caravan in thefe countries, fignifies an affemblage of camels, horfes, mules, men and other animals, who are formed into large bodies for the fake of mutual protection; and as they travel in fome parts for two or three months together over wafte and barren deferts, which yield nothing for the fupport either of man or beaft, are obliged to take all neceffaries with them, and particularly water: it is on thefe occafions that they find the fuperior excellence of the camel to all other animals; not only from its great strength and unwearied perseverance, but from that property it has of sustaining thirst for several days. Those annual caravans which go from Aleppo and Cairo to Mecca, are often composed of thirty or forty thousand people, and are under military government, an officer being appointed by the Grand Signor, called the Emir Hadge, who conducts and commands them; the order of march is regular, and by ranks; the discipline is very exact, and a guard of Janissaries with field-pieces form the escort: they have regular times of marching and halting, which is done by signal. When they take up their ground for the night, tents are pitched, kitchens, cook-shops and coffee-houses are immediately erected, and a large camp is formed; every thing is as quickly packed, and the camels are loaded in the morning to be ready for gun-firing, which puts the whole body in motion. The caravan from Cairo performs its journey to Mecca in forty days, where having staid about a month to celebrate the Hadge, a festival in which both the interests of trade and religion are equally consulted; it returns in the same order, stopping at Medina in the way back, to pay a visit to and make offerings at the shrine of Mahommed, that having been the place of his interment, as Mecca was of his nativity.

The

The zeal shewn by Muffulmen, and the toils and fufferings undergone by them for the fake of paying this compliment to their prophet, are wonderful; they flock to Mecca from all parts of the Mahometan countries, and perform the moft laborious journies: the poorer part of thefe pilgrims, depend on charity for their fupport, which rarely yields them any thing better than a fcanty allowance of bread and water. Vanity, religion, fuperftition and commerce, are the four principal caufes of thefe annual pilgrimages. A Muffulman that has been at Mecca, gains thereby a degree of credit and honor amongft his countrymen, with the term of Hadge added to his name whenever he is fpoke to; his attendance there once at leaft in his life is required by his creed: many vifit it in compliance with vows made at fome time of impending danger, or conditionally on the attainment of a defirable object; others who have lead diffolute lives go there for abfolution, and with an intention to reform; and others for the purpofes of traffick: all fancy themfelves the better for having been there; and from that conviction, perhaps many really become fo.

But to return from Mahommed to my Suez caravan. This being under no regulations, was an irregular and ftraggling body, confifting of about one thoufand camels, and half as many men, and fet out about noon 28th of April, travelling on till eight

eight at night: we then took up our ground; the camels eafed of their burthens, placed themfelves in circles round their food *couchant* with their legs under them, and the men in the fame order formed their meffes: the caravan was in motion by three the next morning, and travelled on without making one fingle halt, even to give the camels water or food, till nine at night: you may from hence be able to form fome conjecture of the power of that animal; the pace we went at, feemed to be nearly four miles an hour, and this was continued for eighteen hours together. My travelling carriage was termed a Kuſhob; to compare fmall things with great, I may fay that it refembles the body of a coach, with an opening between the two feats for the back of the camel on which it is placed longitudinally, fo that one feat hangs on one fide, the other on the other, and on each fits a perfon: I had a canopy over the top, in which I found fingular ufe, as the heat of the fun was intolerable; and though I could not be conveyed in a manner more favorable to my feelings, laying along on mattraſſes and pillows placed over the feat; yet the uneafy motion of the camel, the heat of the weather, and the exceffive drought I experienced, rendered it the moſt unpleafant journey I ever made; I took out my thermometer about two o'clock, and found it 92. but it foon rofe to 96. and fearful that if I kept it longer expofed to this air of fire,

it

it would rife ftill higher, a fight to which my fpirits were not equal, I put it by. Half dead with heat and fatigue, I was confidering whether it would be poffible for me to fupport another day, which I expected we were to pafs in the fame way before we arrived at Cairo, when a Turk who came up from Juddah in the fame fhip with me, rode up to my carriage, afking me *Chooft Bahar-Nile?* Do you fee the Nile? pointing at the fame time to a fpot not very far diftant, telling me immediately after, that we fhould get to the walls of Mezr (the Turkifh name for Cairo,) that night, and go in next morning at fun-rife. I hardly knew how to credit fo joyful a piece of news; but he continuing to affert it ferioufly, I at length believed him, and to me it was like a fentence of reprieve to a condemned man; we accordingly travelled on till near nine, and then came to a fmall village, where we put up for the night, and to my no fmall joy arrived here early the next morning. The diftance from Suez hither is eighty miles, and is always a three days journey for loaded camels, but our's all belonging to Cairo, and being light, as the coffee they came for was not ready, they made their journey in this fhort time that I have mentioned.

Having explained to you the mode of our travelling, it will not require many words to defcribe a country uniformly barren and fandy; fome part of the way lay through a narrow valley, which appeared to be the bed of the canal that was made to join the Mediterranean with the Red Sea, and came into the latter at Suez; a great number of petrified branches of trees, and pieces of wood are met with on the road, with here and there a carcafe on which the vultures prey, and in fome parts a few ftunted fhrubs: every one in thefe journies goes armed, as the caravans are frequently attacked and plundered by the wild Arabs, who ftrip the people, and leave them to perifh on the Defert, a circumftance that I am forry to fay, happened to feveral of our countrymen about three years ago in the following melancholy manner.

A contraband trade had for fome years been carried on by Englifh people from India to Cairo, much to their advantage, and as much to the prejudice of our commerce from thence to Europe: feveral fhips came annually to Suez with cargoes from India; and though there was a Firman of the Grand Signor's, to whom that port belongs, ftrictly forbidding all foreign fhips or chriftians to approach Suez; yet as the Pacha of Cairo and Chief Bey, found their intereft in this illicit trade, they fuffered the Firman to fleep, which it did, till a new Pacha was fent from Conftantinople with ftrict orders to enforce it, whereon the following tragical adventure befell the
Englifh-

Englishmen when they came next to Suez with their accustomed merchandise: not aware of this change of men and measures at Cairo they landed the cargoes of their ships at Suez, paid the duties, loaded the camels, and set off: they travelled on the first day with security, pleasing themselves probably with the visionary wealth which these goods were to produce to them, and little thinking how sad a reverse the next morning's light would occasion: scarce had they moved off the ground where they passed the night, when they were surrounded by a large body of men, plundered, wounded, stripped, and left naked on the Desert, the camels with all their effects, water and provisions being taken off by the robbers: in this piteous plight they consulted what was to be done, the only alternative being whether they should return to Suez, or proceed to Cairo: they imprudently resolved on the latter, whither the distance was double of that to Suez, to which place two only of the company, wiser than the rest, made good their retreat; the others went towards Cairo, at the instance of a Commander of one of the ships, who told them that he knew the way across the Desert, and that by going straight to Cairo, and laying their case before the government, they would stand a better chance of recovering their goods; he gave the first proof how bad his counsel was, for being soon spent with heat and fatigue, he dropped and died. Being without their pilot, the reft had but little chance of finding their way acrofs the Defert, where there is hardly a track; indeed had they known it perfectly, it would have availed them little, naked and expofed to the fcorching beams of an African fun in the month of Auguft, without a drop of water to allay the raging thirft they muft have experienced: all perifhed except one, who arrived fpent and fpeechlefs at fome Arab huts about a league from Cairo; the people there took a great deal of care of him, recovered him a little, and brought him hither; he could fcarcely articulate the name of the perfon to whofe houfe he wifhed to go, who hardly knew him, fo disfigured as he was with his fufferings, which he did not get the better of in a twelvemonth.

You will join with me, no doubt, in condemning the cruelty and weaknefs of a government that executes its laws under the mafk of robbery, and inflicts punifhment in the miferable manner I have above related; and fuch was the mode adopted by the Pacha and Bey to put in force the Firman of the Grand Signor; they themfelves in fact plundered the Caravan, by means of their foldiers whom they fent on this errand, and appropriated the fpoil to their own ufe: they contrived likewife to get poffeffion of the Englifh fhips by an artifice of the fame dark nature, and imprifoned the crews. The government of Cairo,
which

which by openly seizing the effects of the people who came there contrary to the order of the Grand Signor, and contrary to the laws of their own country, would have acted properly, may justly stand taxed with the greatest inhumanity for the conduct they observed; and fearful that it might draw on them the resentment of the English, who with a single frigate could destroy their whole trade in the Red Sea: they obliged all the Englishmen who were then at Cairo to bind themselves, under the penalty of a considerable sum, that no steps should be taken to revenge what had happened, making them find a merchant who resided at Cairo to be surety for them.

No christian ships have come to Suez since this affair: a frigate with dispatches from India came to Cosire about eighteen months ago; but the person charged with them being contraband, was imprisoned here by the Pacha, and sent to Constantinople; for the Firman not only forbids foreign ships, and particularly English, from approaching the port of Suez, but all christians, declaring, "That the sea of Suez was designed for
" the noble pilgrimage of Mecca; and that the
" port thereof is a port of two illustrious cities,
" which are those that make the light of the
" truth to shine, and the law of the prophet; and
" are established to promote religion and justice,

" Mecca the enlightened, and Medina the hon-
" oured; wherefore, it says, let such christians as
" come there, be imprisoned, and their effects
" confiscated; and let no one endeavour to set
them free." I have been thus, you see, ignorant-
ly running into a danger that I was not aware of,
and am here on suspicious ground; but I am told
that having come to Suez in a ship of the country,
and travelling in a private way, I shall escape un-
noticed, however, I promise you, my stay will not
be long unless *per force*; at all risques I must see
the pyramids, and then I hope to quit Cairo, and
shortly after, the land of Egypt.

The inferior station which the Franks, as we
are termed, hold in this country, has already dis-
gusted me against it: among other proofs thereof,
is one of which I daily experience the humiliat-
ing effect, being obliged to ride about the city on
a jack-ass, while the Mussulmen are mounted on
most beautiful Arab horses: it is not only from
being debarred the privilege of riding an horse,
though that is mortifying, but from the general
oppression prevailing here, and the particular
contempt in which the christians are held by these
people, that I am surprized a single one should
be found amongst them. But avarice knows no
prejudices; and man not contented with a sufficiency braves every thing to enrich himself,
esteeming little the sacrifice of each generous
feeling provided wealth does but follow. Adieu.

LETTER

LETTER X.

Cairo, May 7, 1782.

DEAR FRIEND.

I SET out from hence the day before yesterday, accompanied by a party of friends to view the pyramids.

We left Cairo in the afternoon mounted on jack-asses, which convey'd us to Bulac, the port belonging to this place, and there embarked on the Nile for Giza, a voyage of about a league; it stands higher up on the other side of the river, and is opposite to Old Cairo; some travellers have asserted that it is on the scite of the antient Memphis but without just grounds.

Being arrived there we found a house by the water-side prepared for our reception and stored with a plenteous supply of viands and liquors, for which accommodations we were indebted to some

some Italian gentlemen settled at Cairo. Our first business was to find the Scheik of the tribe of Arabs inhabiting the environs of Giza and the pyramids, to let him know our intentions of going thither in the morning and secure his company as a protection to us; accordingly we dispatched an embassador who returned accompanied by the Scheik: some of our party were well acquainted with him as he had attended them before on the like occasion and welcomed him into our presence with a bumper of brandy, to which though a Mussulman he showed no repugnance, but drank near a bottle and after we had adjusted all preliminaries respecting our next day's motions, he retired.

It having been agreed that we should set off at three o'clock in the morning, the Scheik attended by an aid de camp, waited on us at that hour, and being provided with a number of wax candles, necessary for examining the inside of the pyramid, and with all other requisites, we mounted our jack-asses. We arrived at the foot of the pyramids at day-break, by which means they opened to us all at once appearing still more vast in that ambiguous light; and I know not whether my astonishment and satisfaction were greater, on thus suddenly viewing those stupendous fabricks, or afterwards in mi-

nutely

nutely examining their several parts and construction.

After having gazed at them with wonder for some time we prepared to pry into the inmost recesses of the larger pyramid into which only of the three there is an entrance; having lighted our candles we crept in at a small aperture in one of the sides about one fourth of the way up from the base of the pyramid: crawling along on our hands and knees for some way down a sloping and rugged path we came to the lower apartment, where discovering nothing that engaged our curiosity we soon left it, and ascended by a more regular passage up to the great chamber: being arrived there we found it a spacious well-proportioned room, at one end is a tomb or sarcophagos of Granite thought to have contained the body of the prince who built this pyramid as his sepulchral monument: the chamber is lined with granite throughout, the cieling being formed of nine long stones: this room is thirty-six feet long, eighteen feet wide, and twenty feet high; the sarcophagus is seven feet long, four feet wide, and four feet deep. There is a room above this but no way to go up to it. There is likewise supposed to be one below that which we first went into; the way to it is by a deep kind of hole or well which probably leads down to the island, formed by the water of the Nile at the time

time of the annual inundation, according to Herodotus's account, who says that there was a tomb on the island.

Having attentively viewed these inner regions we crept out again half choaked with dust and almost suffocated with the closeness of the air: after a short repose we scaled the sides of the pyramid, which have the appearance of a flight of steps or rows of benches decreasing to a point, for the original smooth and polished surface having mouldered away; the stones placed in regular rows, bear the form I describe, serving by that means as steps to the very summit from whence the view is extensive and noble, taking in the Nile and fertile country on each side of it's banks for a considerable tract, numberless villages, Old Cairo, Giza, the pyramids of Sacara, where are the catacombs, &c. &c. Although there are pyramids without number scattered all over the country, yet these are the three that we call emphatically *the* pyramids, and are here termed *El Haram di Giza* from their vicinity to that place; they stand about nine miles from the banks of the Nile and on the verge of the fertile country, being placed on elevated ground up to the foot of which the water flows on the annual inundation; they are of different sizes: The large one according to Greaves's measurement is 700 feet square, covering

ing about eleven acres of ground; the inclined plane is equal to the base, so that the angles and base make an equi-lateral triangle; the perpendicular height is 500 feet. The apex is thirteen feet square.

The second pyramid stands on as much ground as the first, but is forty feet lower.

The base of the smallest is 300 feet square, and it's perpendicular altitude is eighty feet.

The ruins of their original surfaces lay round the bases of the pyramids and diminish in a slight degree the effect of their grandeur, as in some parts they form a mound covering a quarter of the pyramid which would appear much more noble if cleared of that rubbish; the original surfaces of the two larger appear to have been formed of common stones, but that of the smaller one was composed of beautiful red granite, as may be seen by the broken heaps thereof laying scattered around the base, and by some small portions of the outer crust remaining on the surface. Though an entrance has been discovered only into the larger of the three, yet most probably there is a way into both the others, and likewise apartments in them, since Strabo tells us, that in the middle of the pyramids, there is a stone which may be taken out to open a passage to the tombs: attempts have been made, but without effect, to discover an entrance into the second, a great breach appearing in one of the sides of it.

No certain accounts are given either of the times when, or the kings by whom these extraordinary fabricks were built: Herodotus indeed speaks positively as to the founders of them, but other authors give different accounts, and the whole is uncertain: they are without doubt most wonderful objects considered both with regard to their antiquity, size, and construction; the labour in raising them must have been immense, as they are a solid mass of stones, with only a few small spaces left to form those apartments where the bodies of the kings were laid: the materials were most probably brought from Upper Egypt on floats to the very foot of them. Pliny tells us, that three hundred and sixteen thousand men were employed twenty years in raising the largest, and that the three were compleated in sixty-eight years. Near to these are several smaller pyramids; and round the area, on which the larger ones stand, are a number of recesses and cells in the rock, with hieroglyphick inscriptions over their entrances.

In front of the pyramids towards the Nile, and where the grand approach to them appears
formerly

formerly to have been, is placed the famous figure of the Sphynx, cut out of one solid rock; the increase of the soil and sand has entirely buried the body, the head and neck now only appearing above the ground. The dimensions of this figure according to Pliny, were as follows: the circumference of the head one hundred and two feet, the length of the legs one hundred and thirteen feet, the height from the bottom of the belly to the summit of the head sixty-three feet, and the head and neck twenty-seven feet. It is said to have been the tomb of Amasis; but is more famous on account of the ænigmatical oracles delivered from it to all who went thither to consult it, and from the ambiguous terms in which they were couched, have given rise to the proverbial expression, *Sphynx's riddles*, applied to any thing difficult to be solved. At the top of the head, there was originally an hole, as likewise on the back; from whence issued the answers, dictated by their priests, who were placed within.

The situation of the antient city of Memphis, is determined to have been between the pyramids and the catacombs of Sacara, which are ten miles distant from each other. Although this city was of so great an extent, having been eighteen miles in circuit, yet not the least vestige of it now remains.

We passed the morning in surveying the pyramids, &c. and then rode back through a rich and fertile plain to Giza, from whence we ferried over to the island of Rhoida; it was here that some authors assert Moses to have been found among the rushes by Pharaoh's daughter; whether that was the case or not, I cannot pretend to determine; at present it is famous for a building called the Mikeaz, in which is the Nilometer or pillar placed in the centre of a pool of water of the same level with the river, having different gradations marked on it to determine the daily rise and fall of the Nile: as soon as it begins to rise, the officer superintending the measurement of its altitude, reports the same to the Pacha, and receives handsome presents from him on that event, which is celebrated by publick rejoicings throughout the city; its daily height is likewise constantly proclaimed by publick criers, till it arrives at the wished-for point, when the mound of the canal, designed to distribute its waters throughout the city, is cut with great solemnity and rejoicings, a virgin at the same time being thrown into the river as a present to Father Nile for his annual visit, but it is a virgin of clay placed on the top of the mound, and on cutting it, the figure falls into the river, and is, I suppose, as acceptable to his cold embrace as if it was flesh and blood.

The city of Cairo then becomes a scene of joy and feasting, they receive the river into their streets and squares with the utmost gladness, and boats and barges gaily adorned are seen rowing on lakes and canals, which the day before were dry land; it is then that this city must appear in its greatest glory, at present I can say little for its magnificence, though its size and population are very considerable; the circuit thereof is seven miles, the houses excessively high and streets very narrow, not being wider than our alleys in London, and are always full of people, most of them being mounted, the Turks of fashion on horseback, Christians and Plebeians on jack-asses: to the extreme height of the houses they add every other contrivance possible to exclude the sun, placing over from the tops of the houses on one side of the street to those of the other, canvas strained on frames, whereby the streets are very much darkened and the sun totally excluded, one advantage in this hot country, but then on the other hand, by that means the air is rendered close and suffocating.

In a country where the sky is ever serene and plenty dwells, diffused throughout by the Nile, whose periodical inundations produce rich harvests, of all kinds of grain, and fruits, wafting up from the Mediterranean, the produce of other nations; one is prepared for a
prof-

prospect of universal chearfulness and content, but two curses, the severest that can possibly befall a nation, turn this flattering outside into real misery; the most oppressive system of tyranny in the world, and the destructive ravages made by the plague, are two sources from whence flow the evils of this unfortunate country, the latter is a temporary one; the former invariably subsists, and from it the people know no respite; while the latter rages they lock themselves up in their houses and have no communication with each other, but houses are no refuge against the first, and a despotic Bey seizes on property, and deals out death according to his own pleasure and caprice. I hardly know how to explain to you the form of government here, it is of so strange and complicated a nature: on one hand the Pacha or Vice-Roy sent by the Grand Signor, to whom the country is tributary, claims the sovereignty; on the other, the twenty-four Beys maintain their authority, each of whom exercises an independant power, and by that means there are twenty-five established tyrants, every one of them dispensing justice or injustice according to his pleasure, being under no controul. This government of the Beys is called likewise the Mamaluke government, or government of the slaves, being formed of Georgian slaves, who are sold when young into the families of the Beys and by them trained up to arms, amongst whom, such as

have

have moſt ſpirit and addreſs riſe in their turns to be Beys; little attention being paid to the cultivation of the mind they are extremely ignorant, few of them being able to write or read. The election of a Bey is generally attended with bloodſhed, for as there are many who have pretenſions, the ſword commonly determines the right; Ibrahim Bey has placed himſelf at the head of the government, and by dint of a large army keeps the others in ſome awe, enriching himſelf by rapine and plunder. In ſhort, the ſcene of oppreſſion that exiſts here is a diſgrace to human nature, both in thoſe who practiſe and thoſe who ſuffer it; but the languid and effeminate ſpirit of the native Egyptians, having always made them a prey to foreign maſters, invites that tyranny which it wants the courage to reſiſt. Adieu.

LETTER

LETTER XI.

Cairo,

DEAR FRIEND.

I LITTLE imagined, when I made those observations in my last, respecting the oppression and tyranny of this government, that I should in my own person so soon give proof of what I there advanced; but thus it happened, and the following adventure which I met with, may serve to give you a tolerable idea of Egyptian equity.

In one of my rides about the city, I was met by a party of Turkish soldiers, who accosting *me*, and some European friends who were of my party, said, that by order of their master Mustapha Bey, they were come in search of us, and that they must immediately conduct us to him. We did not at all relish this salutation, and would gladly have been excused the honor of paying a visit to a Bey, but

but having no alternative, we proceeded quietly under their efcort. We were not, you may be fure, extremely comfortable in this fituation; and in our way endeavoured to devine the caufe of it, but in vain: we found we had nothing elfe to do but fubmit patiently, and wait the event. Being arrived at the Bey's palace, my companions were fet at liberty, and *I* only was detained; one of my friends however ftayed with me to act as interpreter, and plead my caufe. We were now ufhered into the prefence chamber, and found this Potentate fitting crofs-legged on a carpet, fmoking a pipe feven or eight feet long; he was a middle-aged man, rather corpulent, had a black and bufhy beard that reached below his breaft, and his countenance was handfome, although ftern and fevere; his myrmidons who were bearded like himfelf, ftood in a circle round him, into the midft of which we were introduced.

The Bey, being informed that I was the perfon whom he had fummoned, furveyed me attentively, and with an imperious tone of voice, pronounced my crime and my fentence in the fame breath, telling me, an Armenian merchant having reprefented to him, that an Englifhman, who had paffed through Cairo two years before, owed him a fum of money, his orders were that I fhould immediately difcharge the debt incurred by my countryman. I heard with aftonifhment this extraordinary charge and verdict, and in reply endeavoured to explain the hardship and injustice of such a proceeding, telling him, that in the first place, I doubted much whether the debt claimed by the Armenian was just, and in the second, supposing that it was, did not consider myself by any means bound to discharge it; but all endeavours to exculpate myself on the principles of reason or justice were totally useless, since he soon removed all my arguments by a short decision, which was, that without further ceremony, I must either consent to pay the money or remain prisoner in his castle. I began then to enquire what the sum was, which the Armenian pretended to be due to him, and found it to be near five hundred pounds, at which price, high as it was, I believe I should have been induced to have purchased my liberty, had not my friend advised me to the contrary, and given me hopes that it might be obtained without it, recommending to me rather to suffer a temporary confinement than submit to so flagrant an extortion. Accordingly I protested against paying the money, and was conducted under a guard into a room where I remained in arrest.

It was about noon, the usual time of dining in this country, and a very good pilau with mutton was served up to me; in short I was very civilly treated in my confinement, but still it was a confinement,

finement, and as such, could not fail of being extremely unpleasant: my only hopes were founded in the good offices of Mr. R―――― an Italian merchant, whose services to me and many of my countrymen, who have been embroiled in affairs of the like nature here, deserve our warmest gratitude.

My apartment was pleasantly situated, with a fine view of the Nile and a rich country; but I should have enjoyed the prospect much more upon another occasion. On a kind of lawn, shaded with trees, in front of the castle, two or three hundred horses stood at picquet, richly caparisoned, belonging to the Bey and his guards. His principal officers and slaves came to visit me, and in talking over my case, they agreed that it was very hard, but to comfort me said, that their master was a very good Prince, and would not keep me long confined. I found several of them pleasant liberal-minded men, and we conversed together very sociably through my Arabian servant, who remained with me.

The people in this country always sleep after dinner till near four o'clock, they then rise, wash and pray; that time of prayer is called by them *Asser*, and is the common hour of visiting; the Beys then give audience, and transact business: Mustapha Bey now sent for me again, and seeming

ing to be in good humour, endeavoured to coax me into payment of the demand he made; but I continued firm in my refusal, on which he changed the subject, and smiling, asked me if I should not like to be a Mussulman, telling me it was much better than being a Christian, and hinted that I should be very well off if I would become one of them, and stay at Cairo, using likewise other arguments to effect my conversion, and all this in a jocular laughing manner: while he was proceeding in his endeavours to bring me over to his faith, two officers came from Ibrahim Bey to procure my release. I have before told you that he is the chief Bey, and luckily Mr. R—— having very good interest with him, had made application in my behalf, and in consequence thereof these two ambassadors were sent to request that Mustapha Bey would deliver me up to them; but he seemed by no means inclinable so to do, and resuming his former sternness of look remained for some time inexorable; till at length wrought on by their entreaties, he consented to let me go, observing at the same time that whenever he had an opportunity of making a little money, Ibrahim Bey always interfered and prevented him; a pretty observation! From which you may infer, that they look upon *us* as fair plunder, and do not give themselves much trouble to find out a pretence on which to found their claims.

The English seem particularly to have been victims to this species of rapine, owing, I believe, to the facility, with which they always submit to it: and many of our wealthy countrymen having returned by this road laden with the spoils of India, these Beys have frequently fleeced them, allured by the temptation of that wealth, which these Nabobs are so fond of displaying: various are the instances of extortions practised on them. You may form an idea of all, when I mention one of a gentleman who passing by Suez in his way to England, that he might not be detained there by the searching of his baggage, prevailed on the Custom-house officers to dispense therewith, and only put their seals on his trunks to exempt them from being visited till his arrival at Cairo, where being come, fatigued with his journey, and impatient to shift himself, he would not wait for the inspection of the officers, but broke the seals to get his clothes, and paid a thousand pounds for the luxury of a clean shirt an hour before he otherwise would have had it.

When I hear of the heavy fines that have been levied on my countrymen in their passage through Egypt, I consider myself very fortunate in being quit for a confinement of only a few hours and fifty pounds given in fees to different people employed in the task of procuring my release.

From

From Muſtapha Bey's palace I was conducted to that of Ibrahim Bey, being attended by an officer of the former who was ſent with me. Ibrahim was ſitting in a ſmall apartment richly furniſhed, ſmoking his pipe, and was accompanied by two other Turks; he appeared to be between forty and fifty years of age, middle-ſized and handſome; he is reckoned a man of ability, indeed he has ſhown himſelf to be ſuch, by having managed with dexterity the complicated machine which he directs. He addreſſed himſelf to Muſtapha Bey's officer, inveighing ſeverely againſt the conduct of his maſter, then turning to me, ſaid that I might depend on his protection during the remainder of my ſtay in that country; and finding that my purpoſe was to go down the Nile and to Alexandria, he gave me a paſſport to exempt me from any trouble or moleſtation I might receive on my paſſage from his General Morad Bey, who was ſtationed on the banks of the Nile with the army, for the purpoſe of raiſing contributions on the country. Having made my proper acknowledgments to this Prince for his civilities I retired not a little rejoiced to have regained my liberty.

Owing to this kind of rapine and extortion practiſed by theſe potentates, and likewiſe to a Firman of the Grand Signor, which forbids European ſhips to approach the port of Suez, this channel

channel of communication betwixt Europe and India has been shut for some years past; a circumstance extremely detrimental to us, since it is by far the most expeditious way of conveying intelligence, and by proper management might still be made use of for that purpose: some presents annually sent by the India Company to my deliverer Ibrahim Bey, who is in fact the king of that country, would ensure safety to their servants, who might pass charged with dispatches; and when you hear that the passage has been made from London to Madrass in sixty-three days by way of Suez, you will be surprized that such an advantage should be overlooked, if possible to be obtained; not that I think it would be adviseable to make it a common road for passengers, or permit any other ships to go to Suez, but small packet boats for the purpose of conveying dispatches; for otherwise a door would be opened to a contraband trade, which would prove extremely prejudicial to the commerce of the India Company, and the revenue of our government.

Mr. R―――― received me on my return to his house with the strongest expressions of joy and friendship, and I endeavoured to testify to him with equal warmth how sensible I was of the service he had rendered me. This gentleman who possesses a mind far too liberal for the country in which he resides, has been settled here for many years,

years, and acquired an handsome fortune, though he has frequently been squeezed by the Beys; at present he finds the advantage of paying one, to be protected against the extortions of the others: he is extremely attached to the English, and has often been of great service to them in this city.

Hadge Cossim, who is a Turk, and one of the richest merchants in Cairo had interceded in my behalf with Ibrahim Bey, at the instance of his son, who had been on a pilgrimage to Mecca, and came from Juddah in the same ship with me. The Father in celebration of the son's return, gave a most magnificent fête on the evening of the day of my captivity, and as soon as I was released, sent to invite me to partake of it, and I accordingly went. His company was very numerous, consisting of three or four hundred Turks, who were all sitting on sophas and benches, smoking their long pipes; the room in which they were assembled, was a spacious and lofty hall, in the centre of which was a band of musick composed of five Turkish instruments, and some vocal performers; as there were no ladies in the assembly, you may suppose, it was not the most lively party in the world, but being new to me, was for that reason entertaining.

Both

Both on account of my nation, and my recent adventure with the Bey, I was a kind of sight to them, and they asked me numberless questions, at the same time being extremely civil, and several of them, as a great compliment, taking their pipes out of their mouths, and offering them to me to smoke; although the indelicacy of this custom was somewhat disgusting, yet in conformity to their manners, I took their pipes, smoked two or three whiffs, and returned them; they look upon it as the civillest thing they can do to a stranger or visitor, to offer him the dish of coffee they themselves are sipping, or the pipe they are smoking, which it would be the height of ill manners in any one to refuse. Our supper was served at twelve o'clock, and consisted of sweet-meats, pastry and sherbets, served on silver waiters placed on the carpet, around which we formed ourselves in different parties of five or six in each: we did not continue long at table, and immediately as our repast was finished, the company broke up.

In walking home through the streets, I could not but observe the good police which seems to prevail here; each district or ward of the city is shut up separately within gates, and no one is ever suffered to stir out after dark without a lanthorn, on pain of being taken up and imprisoned;

a patrole of Janiffaries goes the rounds frequently in the night; fo that I fhould think with thefe precautions few enormities are ever commmitted.

My late adventure has made me particularly impatient to quit this country, where perfonal property and perfonal liberty are held fo light; and I fhall accordingly fet off to-morrow morning, having engaged a boat, and made all other neceffary preparations for my paffage down the Nile to Rofetta; and I hear that I am not likely to meet with Morad Bey's army, as he has left that branch of the river along which I fhall pafs, fo that I flatter myfelf I fhall meet with no further hindrance or interruption in my journey. Adieu.

LETTER

LETTER XII.

Alexandria.

DEAR FRIEND.

THE paffage down the Nile from Cairo to Rofetta is charming: the verdure, fertility, and abundance of the Delta of Egypt highly pleafing.

By that name the Romans diftinguifhed the country laying between the outward forks of the river, into which it divides a few miles below Cairo, and makes with the fea a figure refembling the Greek letter Δ. From thefe two principal branches go feveral others, interfecting the country that lays between; and this bounteous river, after fcattering plenty over the land, during a courfe of many hundred miles, empties itfelf into the fea by feven mouths: the two moft confiderable are thofe of Damiatta and Rofetta; the former was

was the Oſtium Pathmeticum of the antients; the latter, the Oſtium Bolbitinum.

As the pyramids may juſtly be eſteemed the moſt wonderful of all the works of art, ſo the Nile may be conſidered as the greateſt natural curioſity in this country. Nature to ſupply her parſimonious diſtribution of water from the heavens upon this land, has ordained an annual overflow of the river, to water and enrich it, ſo that perpetual plenty and verdure here flouriſh without the aſſiſtance of the clouds. Tibullus with regard to Egypt ſays,

> Te propter nullos tellus tua poſtulat imbres
> Arida nec pluvio ſupplicat herba Jovi.
> It's flocks to fatten and to ſwell it's grain,
> This land from heav'n aſks not refreſhing rain.

The Nile is ſaid to riſe in the twelfth degree of North Latitude, at the foot of a great mountain, in the kingdom of Goyana, in Abyſſinia, but this is rather matter of conjecture than certainty, no exact accounts having hitherto been given of its ſource, but ſuppoſing it to be ſomewhere near the part I mentioned, its courſe being north and ſouth, and emptying itſelf into the ſea in the thirty-firſt degree of North Latitude, the whole extent thereof muſt be about one thouſand two hundred miles.

The

COAST OF ARABIA FELIX, &c.

The annual rise which it experiences is owing to periodical rains that fall in Abyssinia; the river begins to swell at Cairo and in lower Egypt towards the latter end of June, and rising gradually till the middle of September, decreases afterwards during the months of October and November: the height which it attains varies in different years, and the plenty or scarcity of the crops is determined thereby, when it rises to sixteen peeks (about thirty-two feet) the chalitz, which distributes the water through the city of Cairo, is opened, then, and not till then, the Grand Signor is entitled to his tribute, nor do they wish to see it much higher than that point, since one extreme is as fatal to this country as the other, if there is a deficiency of water, many lands are deprived of the benefit thereof, if there is a super-abundance, it retires not soon enough for them to sow their corn. The river at this time spreading itself over the country, on each side of its bed for several leagues, appears like a sea; whatever parts lay so remote as to be out of reach of the inundation, are watered by canals and partly from its own beneficence, partly from what is borrowed of it by these canals, so much is expended in its course that it has been conjectured, that not a tenth part of its water reaches the sea.

The appearance which Egypt prefents at that feafon of the year, muft be very fingular and curious to one who afcends an high building, and difcovers a vaft expanfe of water all around with towns and villages rifing out of the flood, here and there a caufey, and numberlefs groves and fruit-trees whofe tops only are vifible. When the waters retire they leave a vaft quantity of fifh on the land, and at the fame time, what is much more valuable, a flime which acts as manure and fertilizes the fields. By this annual addition of foil Egypt has been very much raifed and enlarged in the courfe of years, and many places are now inland which were formerly clofe to the fea, fuch particularly is Damiatta; and as the mud of the Nile extends for fome leagues into the fea, and accumulates every year, this country by little and little annually increafes.

The Arts, Mythology, and Natural Hiftory of Antient Egypt, form a fubject fo worthy the attention and ftudy of the curious, that they cannot have efcaped your's; I need not therefore dwell on the fuperftition or fingular worfhip formerly practifed here, addreffed to bulls, ferpents, crocodiles, birds, fifh of different kinds, and even the pulfe and roots of the garden, all which they deified. I need not tell you that amongft other ufeful inventions for which

plant

we are indebted to this country, is paper, made of a plant called Papyrus, or Byblos, that grew near Memphis. You well know the miraculous effects ascribed by the poets to the plant Lotus, this was an Egyptian root, and used by way of bread.

I will not recapitulate to you subjects you are well acquainted with, but return to Rosetta, a very pleasant city standing close to the Nile, in the midst of gardens and orange groves. I took mules from thence, and riding close by the sea for about fifteen miles, came to the most westerly branch of the Nile, crossing it a little above the Ostium Canopicum, after which appeared the castle of Bekier, standing close to the sea on the scite of the antient Canopus, a city notorious for the debauchery and dissoluteness that prevailed there; travelling on a few miles further, through a sandy country thickly planted with date-trees, I came to the ruins of the antient Nicopolis, situated on an hill; this city was built by Augustus, and received its name in commemoration of a victory gained by him over Anthony; a league more brought me hither.

The city of Alexandria founded by Alexander the Great, and afterwards so much admired and adorned by the Romans, the residence of Cleopatra, and refuge of Anthony, once famous for its magnificence, luxury, and learning, is now become an undistinguishable heap of ruins; baths, palaces, porticos, and amphitheatres lay promiscuously jumbled together. The savage rage of the Saracens when they took it, has reduced it to this miserable state; but a circumstance more to be lamented than any other, was the destruction of the famous Ptolemean Library, containing one hundred thousand volumes. On taking the city, the general sent to the Caliph, to know his orders respecting those books, who returned for answer, by all means to burn them, for if they were agreeable to the Alcoran they were superfluous, and if contrary to it, impious; accordingly the Mussulmen applied them to the purpose of heating their baths, and it was six months before they were consumed.

Pompey's pillar is an object the most striking of any now extant; it is situated on an eminence a quarter of a mile to the southward of the walls, and is of red granite: the height of the shaft is ninety feet, and diameter thereof nine feet, the whole height of the column is one hundred and fourteen feet, the capital is of the Corinthian order; I must not omit mentioning to you the manner by which some English masters of ships contrived to get to the top of it; they flew a kite over the pillar in such a direction, that when

the

the string was loosed to let it fall and the kite came to the ground, the string lay across the top of the pillar, by means of which they passed ropes over, and making shrouds the same as to the mast of a ship, they went up triumphantly, drinking a bowl of punch on the summit, and discovering that there had formerly been a pedestrian statue on it, a piece of the foot remaining.

There are two obelisks called Cleopatra's, having perhaps been part of the ornaments of her palace, which stood near the sea side, one of them is overthrown and lays half buried in the sand, the other is still standing, and is sixty-three feet high, on each side are hieroglyphicks. They shew some subterranean apartments, and call them Catacombs, but I think it more probable from their form, that they were baths, and the increase of the ground occasioned by the ruins, has buried them; so great has been the havock that there is not another pile remaining, sufficiently entire, to mark its original form or purpose, even the Pharos, reckoned one of the wonders of the world, has nothing now to represent it but a Turkish fort built on the same spot, and probably out of its ruins.

Many curious antiques, such as medals, rings, and small statues, have occasionally been picked up up amongst the ruins, and numberless others of value might be found could permission be obtained to dig, but so jealous are these people of the Christians, who they suppose have no other view in visiting these places but to find hidden treasures, that it is often dangerous to look at them.

The present city does not stand on the scite of the antient Alexandria, but on a portion of ground that was called the Hepta-Stadium, and lay without the walls; it is a kind of Peninsula situated between the two ports, that to the westward was called by the antients the Portus Eunostus, now the Old Port, and is by far the best, Turkish vessels only are allowed to anchor there: the other called the New Port is for the Christians; at the extremity of one of the arms of which stood the famous Pharos.

Historians tell us that Alexander's body was embalmed, and buried in this city in a coffin of gold, which (as one can easily suppose) was taken away and it was put into one of glass, being preserved therein so late as to the time of Augustus, who took a view of it in that state, adorned it with a golden crown, and wept over it.

I have

I have now been here near a month, a daily witnefs of the fad revolution that has taken place in men, manners, arts, and learning at Alexandria; too long a time to dwell on an unpleafing picture. I embark to-morrow on board a fhip bound to Tunis, which will pafs by Malta, and and fet me on fhore at that ifland; the quarantine being fhorter than at any of the ports of Italy. I fhall be happy to communicate to you, the account of my arrival there. Adieu.

LETTER

LETTER XIII.

Lazaret of Leghorn, August 15, 1782.

DEAR FRIEND.

BEING at length landed in Europe I delay not a moment to impart an event so pleasing, and at the same time give you the sequel of my wanderings.

I embarked on board a neutral vessel at Alexandria, the master of which instead of shaping a direct course for the port he was bound to, run up amongst the islands of the Archipelago, according to the practice of those Mediterranean sailors, who always keep the land close aboard, and on the appearance of a black cloud make for the first harbour that presents itself; had he carried me the tour of the Grecian islands and set me on shore at those we passed, I could have borne more patiently the tediousness of our voyage, but I confess that a distant view did not sufficiently

ficiently compenfate for that unpleafing circumftance; the only one which I had an opportunity of vifiting was Rhodes, where we put in for a day or two.

The famous Coloſſus now no longer beſtrides the entrance of the harbour, no beautiful villas adorn its ſhores, no palaces grace the city, no Romans now refide here; its natural beauties however ſtill remain, but in the hands of Turks who are not much given to improvement, and practife no arts but thoſe of oppreſſion, as the Chriſtian inhabitants feverely feel. The town ſtill bears the marks of that memorable fiege it once fuſtained, when the knights of St. John of Jerufalem, headed by Villers de Lifle Adam, Grand Mafter, made a gallant ſtand againſt the arms of Solyman the Magnificent, who befieged the place with two hundred thoufand men, and four hundred ſhips; the brave garrifon confifting only of five thoufand foldiers, and fix hundred knights, was, after a fix months fiege, during which they had made frequent fallies, and given incredible proofs of valour, obliged to capitulate from a total want of provifions and every kind of ſtore; the knights afterwards fettled at Malta, given to them by the Emperor Charles V. as fome kind of recompence for having with-held his affiſtance in fo critical a conjuncture.

The

The surrounding country appeared extremely pleasant and fruitful, but the shortness of our stay did not allow me to penetrate into it, or even visit the spot where that city stood which the Romans so much admired, and where they used to pass their time in elegant retirement; it was situated about a league to the northward of the present city, on a bank sloping down to the sea, but few vestiges of it now remain. There is a convent of Catholick Monks at Rhodes, to whose hospitality all Christians who touch there are much indebted.

After leaving this island we steered for the coast of Candia, the antient Crete, and on approaching it discovered a very lofy mountain, that I conjectured to be mount Ida; we sailed from one extremity of this island to the other, and were often very near the shore. From Candia we stretched on to the Capes of the Morea and the isle of Serigo, formerly Cythera, and then quitting the Archipelago, stood over towards Malta; but as we had lost sight of land for a few days, and did not keep the best of reckonings, we missed that island, and contrary to my wishes and expectations, I was carried on to Tunis, on the coast of Barbary.

In approaching that city we sailed up a deep bay, answering exactly the description given of it by Virgil, in his Æneid.

Est

,Eft in feceffu longo locus ; infula portum
Efficit objectu laterum : quibus omnis ab alto
Frangitur inq. finus fcindit fefe unda reductos.

Within a long recefs there lies a bay,
An ifland fhades it from the rolling fea,
And forms a poft fecure for fhips to ride,
Broke by the jutting land on either fide.
DRYDEN.

We came to an anchor at the upper end thereof, near the caftle of the Goletta, and paffed in the boat through a narrow canal into an extenfive bafon, on which ftands Tunis; the water in it is fo fhallow, that we were frequently aground in our paffage up to the city, which is twelve miles diftant from the road where the fhips lay.

Though I can fay nothing in favour of the town, yet the country is pleafant and abounds in a great variety of productions, moft of which are fhipped off for Europe. Trade and piracy here enrich the people, the latter they carry on very fuccefsfully againft all the petty ftates of the Mediterranean, whofe naval force is not fufficiently powerful to crufh them; they go in fmall gallies mounting a few fwivels, to the number of fifty or fixty men in each, armed with firelocks and cutlaffes, and as thefe veffels fail extremely faft, and alfo row twenty or thirty oars, they are equally prepared to efcape or overtake as occafion may require. Among other valuable

valuable articles brought in by the Corsairs, are their prisoners; who are sold in the public market, and fetch very high prices; these poor wretches then groan under a miserable slavery during the remainder of their lives, except such as not being scrupulous in matters of faith, prefer Mahometan liberty to Christian bondage and become Mussulmen. But I am told that the slaves are treated much better at Tunis than any where else, indeed the people themselves are far more civilized than those of the other Barbary states, most likely owing to the great commerce and intercourse they have with Europeans.

I own I was much struck with the liberty there enjoyed, and the security with which one might travel about the country, circumstances very different from what I had met with in Arabia and Egypt, where, if you stir but out of a town you are sure to be stripped, and are lucky to escape unwounded and alive, but at Tunis you may take your horse, and stroll from one end of the kingdom to the other, which I should certainly have done, if my constitution had been equal to combat with the heat of the climate; conceive what it must have been when we shut up windows and doors to exclude the air that in other countries we court, and when the thermometer exposed thereto rose higher than 100.

The

The Bagrada, Utica and Zowan are deserving notice, but my attention was confined to the scite and ruins of the famous city of Carthage, which, from the lustre it once maintained, the generals it produced, and the three long and bloody wars it sustained against its more successful rival Rome; add to all these circumstances, that it is the scene of the most interesting part of the Æneid, I could not but venerate as classick ground.

The English conful, to whose politeness and hospitality I was much indebted, carried me to his country house at Merfa, about ten miles from Tunis, standing on the scite of part of the antient city of Carthage; I spent a few days there with him very agreeably, and in the cool of the mornings and evenings amused myself with strolling about and tracing as well as I could the ruins and extent of that famous city: but the dreadful sentence pronounced against it in the Roman senate, has been so fully accomplished, that nothing now remains to give one an idea of it's antient grandeur: piles of ruins may be seen all along the shore from the castle of the Goletta to Cape Carthage, and so on to Cape Gomert; and several appear under water, having the form of walls or wharfs, which the sea, by encroaching on the land has overwhelmed. Antient authors tell us, that this city was eighteen leagues in circuit; but that space is now covered with corn-fields, vineyards, and gardens, with here and there a mafs of ruins appearing.

The Byrfa retains still the appearance of its former strength, the ground falling every way with great declivity from the summit, on which there is a ruin something in the shape of a tower: subterranean vaults are to be seen in every part of the country thereabouts; the most perfect and curious remains of antiquity, are the cisterns placed on an eminence to the northward of the Byrfa; these are large canals, that were designed as reservoirs to supply the city with water: there are seventeen of them, each being one hundred feet in length, twenty in breadth, and ten deep; at one corner is a ruin, appearing to have been a dome, and most probably there was the like at each of the other three corners; the aquæduct which brought the water to them was ninety miles in extent, and begun at the foot of a lofty mountain called Zowan; it may be traced all the way by its ruins, and in some places the arches still remain entire.

Several villages are scattered about on the antient scite of this city, viz. El Merfa close by the sea, Melcha under ground, those subterranean apartments in which the people live, having formerly been vaults to the Carthaginian houses that stood there: Darilfhut near the Goletta, and Seedy

Seedy Mosaid standing on the promontory called Cape Carthage, it is a pleasant hill covered with vineyards and plantations of olive trees, &c. but being sacred on account of a Mahometan saint buried there, must not be profaned by christian feet; a *propos* of those saints I ought to inform you, that the Mussulmen canonize those to whom nature has denied reason, paying them the greatest respect when alive, and venerating them when dead; they walk about stark naked, and whatever extravagancies they commit, are overlooked.

You will not be surprized that so little now remains of what was once so vast a city, when you consider that the Romans after plundering, razed it, and that the fire which consumed it, lasted seventeen days. Two other cities were afterwards built near the same spot, notwithstanding the edict of the Roman senate, forbidding any revival of the name of Carthage, once so odious to them; but both have shared the fate of the first, and few traces remain of either.

The river Bagrada famous in history for that serpent of astonishing size slain on its banks by the army of Regulus, falls into the sea near Porta Farina, twenty miles to the northward of Cape Carthage; Utica is also situated on it, whither Cato retired and killed himself.

I cannot

I cannot descend from this great and interesting subject to describe the modern state of that country formerly so eminent, or quit even the ruins of antient Carthage, to dwell on the present royal palaces of Bardo and Manubia, looked on in Barbary to be *chef d'œuvres* of art and magnificence; all comparison between the present and past would be painful either to relate or hear, let me embark therefore at that port from whence Hanno, Hannibal and Hamilcar once led their victorious fleets and armies, and going on board a Ragusan snow, pursue my voyage along the coasts of Sardinia and Corsica to this port, where, although a temporary prisoner, I submit patiently to my captivity, since it is a condition annexed to my arrival in Europe, happy to have exchanged the barbarous climes of Asia and Africa, for regions of taste, pleasure and refinement. Adieu.

TRANSLATION

TRANSLATION

OF A

FIRMAN of the *Ottoman Porte*.

IT is the Grand Signor's pleasure that no Christian vessel come to Suez, or trade from Juddah to Suez openly or secretly. The sea of Suez was designed for the noble pilgrimage of Mecca; such as assist in giving a passage to Christian vessels, or connive at it, or use not their utmost endeavours to prevent it, are traitors to their religion, and to their Sovereign, and to all Mussulmen; and such as have the presumption to transgress, will find their punishment both in this and the other world; and this express command is on account of the important affairs of state, and of religion. Do as we command you, with fervor
and

and zeal, let our royal mandate be thus pronounced of which this is the tenor.

(Here follow the names of the Pachas, Beys, and Governors, to whom the Firman is addressed.)

Be it known that the port of Suez, where the ships anchor, is a port of two honoured cities, which are those that make the light of the truth to shine and the law of the prophet, and are established to promote religion and justice, Mecca the enlightened, and Medina the honoured; and may God enoble them to the end of the world.

It hath never been customary for any ships of foreign nations, or for the children of darkness to come into the sea of Suez, nor for English or other ships, to bring their cargoes beyond Juddah, till lately, when in the time of Ali Bey, a small English vessel or two came to Suez, with presents from a person unknown, for the said Bey, and informed him, that they were come to seek a freight; and having once come there, the English have therefore thought, that they could at all times do the same, and they have come to Suez with their ships laden with piece goods of India and other effects, in the time of the deceased Mahommed Bey, Father of Gold, who was likewise deceived by avarice, some people pointing out to him certain advantages arising there-

therefrom; so that, English and other ships have repeatedly come to the port of Suez.

These matters have come to our royal ears, which we hold to be contrary to the policy of our kingdom, and to religion; and we do command that from henceforwards, none of the Christians come to or approach Suez, hereby absolutely forbidding them. We have time after time, commanded them to return to their country, and have informed their ambassador thereof, enjoining him to write to his sovereign to forbid these ships to come to Suez, it being contrary to custom, and to our royal pleasure; and the ambassador has shown to us the answers he has received from his Court, and from the India Company, wherein is declared, that all travellers and merchants are strictly forbidden to approach or pass by Suez; therefore if any should disobey this order, let them be imprisoned, and their effects confiscated, and let an account thereof be sent to our illustrious Porte.

We have informed ourselves from the wise men, and those who study history, and have heard what has passed in former times from the dark policy of the Christians, who will undergo all fatigues travelling by sea and land, and they take drawings of the countries through which they pass, and keep them, that by help thereof, they may

may make themselves masters of the kingdoms as they have done in India and other places. Memorials have likewise come to us on the part of the Xerif of Mecca, the much honoured, representing, that these Christians above-named, not contented with their traffick to India, have taken coffee and other merchandize from Yemen, and carried it to Suez, to the great detriment of our port of Juddah.

Seeing therefore what has happened, and our royal indignation being excited; particularly when we consider how things are in India, by means of the Christians, who for many years have undergone long voyages, and at first declaring themselves to be merchants, meaning no harm or treachery, deceived the Indians, who were fools, and did not understand their subtlety and craft, and thus have taken their cities, and reduced them to slavery. And in the time of Talmon, with like craft, they entered the city of Damascus, under the mask of merchants, who do no harm, and paying the full duties or even more. At that time it happened, that there were differences between Talmon and Labbason, and the Christians turned them to their advantage, and made themselves masters of Damascus and Jerusalem, and kept possession of them for an hundred years, when Saladin appeared, to whom God give glory, and freed Damascus and Jerusalem, killing

killing the Christians without number. Besides, it is well known, how great an hatred they bear to Mussulmen on account of their religion, and seeing with an evil eye Jerusalem in our hands. Those therefore, who connive at the Christians coming to Suez, will be punished by God both in this and the other world. Permit by no means, Christians or other ships to pass and repass by Suez, but take such as assist them secretly, and chastise them as they deserve.

Our royal sovereignty is powerful, and this is our Royal Mandate, when any Christian ships, and particularly the English shall come to the port of Suez, imprison the captains, and all the people, since they are rebels and offenders both against their own government and our's, according to the declaration of their ambassador, and according to the answer sent from his Court; and they deserve imprisonment and confiscation of their effects, which let them find, and let no one endeavour to set them free.

F I N I S.

www.ingramcontent.com/pod-product-compliance
Lightning Source LLC
Chambersburg PA
CBHW020105170426
43199CB00009B/405